REALISTIC THEOLOGY

REALISTIC
THEOLOGY

WALTER MARSHALL HORTON

LONDON
HODDER AND STOUGHTON LIMITED
MCMXXXV

TABLE OF CONTENTS

PREFACE

THIS book may be regarded as an answer to the question raised by John Bennett in a searching article last fall: "After Liberalism—What?" I have kept Bennett's article at my elbow throughout the writing of the book and references to it will be found in almost every chapter. I agree with substantially everything in it, except its fear of the rising emphasis upon the church. It seems to me, as to Bennett, that liberalism *as a system of theology* has collapsed and must be replaced, but that it stood and still stands for precious truths and values which must not be allowed to die. Like him, I see no great hope in any of the well-recognized schools of theology now in the field; but I sense a great ground-swell of new life in the general "realistic" tendency of our times, which I believe is capable of furnishing the guiding principles of the new theology that is required. Realism like liberalism has its perils, as I endeavor to show; but in what Paul Tillich calls a "belief-ful Realism" I see hope of a new statement of Christian faith, in which former conservatives and former liberals may find they have more in common than they used to suppose. With Reinhold Niebuhr, I find that the attempt to face the exigencies of our times is driving me "politically to the left, theologically to the right" —thus bringing me into simultaneous relations of sympathy with Christian orthodoxy on the one hand and with social radicalism on the other. I am convinced that the disease of our civilization is deep-rooted, and only radical measures can hope to cure it; but I find in traditional Christianity a deep-going diagnosis of our human predicament and a vast reservoir of divine power and wisdom, without which no program of social change can possibly succeed.

The invitation extended to me by the Andover-Newton Theological School to give the Greene lectures in April of this year, has afforded me an opportunity of putting these new gropings and insights into presentable shape; and the invitation of Union Theological Seminary to address the Annual Ministers' Conference in July has enabled me to submit my ideas to a second round of criticism before publishing them. I have to express my thanks to the Andover-Newton faculty and students for many courtesies extended to me during my stay there, and to many friendly critics, young and old, who have enabled me to correct my thought at certain points. I am very conscious still of the temerity and possible error of many of my statements; but I believe the times require bold speaking, and I must not delay my utterance too long, lest my words fail to meet the precise situation for which they were framed. So I say to my little book, in the old phrase, "go with God," and I pray that it may be used for the kindling of the religious renewal we so desperately need.

My thanks are due to the editors of the *Intercollegian* and the *New Yorker*, to Mr. Edmund Wilson, Mr. John Gordon and Rev. John Haynes Holmes, and to the following publishing houses, for permission to quote copyrighted materials: Yale University Press, The Macmillan Company, The Fleming H. Revell Company and Harper & Brothers.

New York, August 3, 1934

REALISTIC THEOLOGY

CHAPTER I

THE DECLINE OF LIBERALISM AND THE RISE OF REALISM

I. THE DECLINE OF LIBERALISM

No ONE who has kept in touch with the recent trend of religious thought and discussion can fail to be aware that something calamitous has been happening to the type of theology known as "liberalism."

Fifteen years ago, at the close of the World War, liberalism was still self-confident and aggressive. Strong in the faith that all truth and all value belonged to a single harmonious system, of which the religious insights of the Bible and the guiding conceptions of modern science and philosophy were mutually consistent parts, liberal theologians were convinced that the great task of Christian thought was that of "restating" the Christian Gospel in terms "acceptable to the modern mind." When the fundamentalists took fright at some of the consequences of this attempt to reconcile Christ and Culture, the liberals denounced them as "obscurantists," clinging to "outmoded thought-forms"; and when they were in turn denounced as "modernists," many of them accepted the terms of opprobrium as a badge of honor, correctly describing their conviction that it was possible to be at once thoroughly modern and thoroughly Christian.

Today, the self-assurance of the liberals seems to

have melted away. Instead of pursuing the retreating hosts of "obscurantism," in the name of light and truth, they now stand beating their own breasts and lamenting their errors. Instead of repelling the harsh criticisms of the fundamentalists, they are now criticizing themselves, just as severely and ten times as destructively. A teacher in a well-known liberal seminary said to me recently that hardly a sermon had been preached or a lecture delivered within its walls for a year which did not at some point go out of its way to take a crack at liberalism—and that in spite of the fact that most of these sermons and lectures were thoroughly liberal in all their presuppositions! Professor John Bennett is right, I believe, when he says that "The most important fact about contemporary American theology is the disintegration of Liberalism."[1] Disintegration is not too strong a word. The defeat of the liberals is becoming a rout. Harried by the fundamentalists on the right flank and the humanists on the left, their position has long been a difficult one; but it could be maintained as long as their own morale remained unimpaired. Now their morale has cracked, rebellion and desertion are rife within their ranks, and the greater part of their forces are ready to "flee when no man pursueth."

What has happened to destroy the self-confidence of the liberals? That is not altogether easy to determine. Doubtless a part of the explanation is to be seen—as has just been suggested—in the difficult position into which they have fallen, between the conservative de-

[1] *Christian Century*, November 8, 1933 (Vol. L, No. 45, pp. 1403-1406).

fenders of Christian tradition and the radical proponents of complete "experimentalism" in religion. So long as the liberals were permitted to make their own interpretation of the Christian Gospel—as, for example, in Harnack's famous lectures on "What is Christianity?" —and so long as they were permitted to draw their own conclusions from their "modern" methods and principles, they found little difficulty in harmonizing the two. When the more scholarly fundamentalists, such as Professor Machen, pointed out the real divergencies between the liberal Gospel and the New Testament Gospel, it was still possible to profess allegiance to the "abiding experiences" which underlay the outmoded "categories" of early Christianity, and rethink these experiences in modern terms. But when the humanists appeared upon the scene, with their Gospel of salvation by scientific research and coöperative effort, the dilemma of liberalism became acute. The humanists professed to be the real moderns, and it must be admitted that their position represented, in some respects, a logically consequent outworking of principles to which the liberals themselves had appealed in their critique of fundamentalism. If now they refused to carry out these principles to the bitter end, what reasons could they give for their refusal? Had they not sworn to "follow the truth, if it led them over Niagara"? Was it honorable or courageous of them to desert the truth and make for the shore, as soon as they felt the pull of the current and the roar of the Falls? Was there in fact any shore to which they could return, now that they had cut loose from churchly tradition and infallible revelation, and committed themselves to the outcome of free inquiry, whatever it might be?

These are embarrassing questions, and they are not imaginary ones. More than once, in recent years, I have had just such indignant questions put to me by earnest religious thinkers of the younger generation, whose hopes of a great new age for religion had been kindled by the prophetic trumpet-blasts which came from the liberal camp a dozen years ago, but who now felt personally betrayed and cheated when the liberal movement refused to march on into the Promised Land of humanism. Dr. Fosdick—who for some reason is always selected to serve as sin-bearer for liberalism—appears to these young humanists as Wordsworth appeared to young Browning and Shelley after his defection from the principles of the French Revolution: as a "Lost Leader," deserting "to the rear and the slaves," from sheer failure of nerve, just when his blade was thought to be uplifted to strike the decisive blow for freedom.[2]

It is not hard to understand the disappointment and indignation of such impetuous minds when they see their erstwhile leaders beginning to draw back; and yet

[2] As a matter of fact, Dr. Fosdick has been for years a severe critic of the liberal theology. It used to be his habit to prescribe to his homiletics class the writing of a sermon on "The Perils of Liberalism." In *Christianity and Progress*, he subjects the favorite liberal dogma, of progress, to a drastic overhauling; while in his recently published volume of sermons, *The Hope of the World* (1933), he exhibits what I should call distinctly "realistic" tendencies. See especially the Christmas sermon on "Beautiful Ideals and Brutal Facts," pp. 214-221.

I venture to suggest that their bitter emotion springs from a superficial diagnosis of the reasons for the liberal recoil from humanism. Fear of the unknown may have influenced the rank and file, but what brought the liberal leaders to a halt before the spectacle of humanism was something more than fear. It was a sudden doubt as to the validity of some of their own guiding principles, which seemed to be finding in humanism a sort of systematic *reductio ad absurdum*; and this doubt was rooted in a sudden perception of the historical relativity of their whole undertaking. They now began to see that in their endeavor to "modernize" and "liberalize" Christianity they had brought it into a compromising alliance with the peculiar presuppositions, prejudices and illusions of a particular type of civilization (Western industrialism) and even of a particular section of society (the middle class). Since this particular type of civilization has begun to suffer a decline, and since this particular section of society has passed its apogee, the liberal theology has now fallen beneath the same sentence of doom which it so often pronounced upon older systems of theology: O irony of ironies, its "thought-forms" have become "outmoded"! The thoroughness with which liberalism did its work has been its own undoing; having completely assimilated the characteristic ideas of a particular era in history, it was foredoomed to perish with the passing of the era.

It is no longer possible to doubt, in this year of our Lord 1934, that we are really standing, in the arresting phrase of Karl Barth, *"Zwischen den Zeiten"*—"between eras." So long as the post-war debauch of individualism and self-expression lasted, it was natural to hope that when we sobered down after our petulant fling, we might take up the tasks of civilization again at the point where the war interrupted us. Now that five years of economic stagnation and social distress have cleared our heads and sharpened our vision, we see plainly enough that we can never return, in any sense, to pre-war "normalcy." We are sure now that neither the war, nor the emotional storm that followed it, nor the great economic depression that resulted from it was a mere episode. They were the first tremendous indications of a great turn in the stream of history, the beginnings of a new era to which as yet we have no chart or compass. The "First World War," as Laurence Stallings calls it, was only the curtain-raiser in this new drama. The Jazz Decade, with its fantastic mood of bitter bravado, was only a "Strange Interlude" with which our minds were temporarily distracted while the stage carpenters were hammering away, setting the scenery for the main performance which has just begun, and whose plot so far is hard to unravel.

If it is impossible to describe the new era in advance, it is at least possible to describe the era which is now at an end, and note the direction in which the line of change seems to be tending. It was an era of mounting faith in man's ability to control his own destiny through creative intelligence, and to make a heaven on earth with the aid of science and machinery. The material basis for this faith may be discerned in the steadily mounting prosperity of the Western industrial nations—

unequally distributed, to be sure, and resting upon imperialistic exploitation of less fortunate peoples, but
sufficiently widespread to give a kindly and hopeful
outlook upon life to the great mass of the population in
America and in Western Europe. If this "era of good
feeling" was not so evidently a happy one for the dispossessed American Indians or King Leopold's black
subjects in the Belgian Congo, or even for the
"Hunkies" who worked in the steel mills of Pitts-
burgh, it was nevertheless obvious to the members of
the great middle class, from which Protestant Christianity has been mainly recruited, that they lived in a highly
rational and moral universe, where virtue and industry
were sure to find their reward. In so far as they were
conscious of any lack of equity in the distribution of
privileges, they were sincerely desirous—up to a certain point—of doing something to redress the balance;
and they gave out of their comfortable superfluity to
an astonishing variety of charitable, humanitarian and
missionary causes. Through education and the growth
of "understanding" between nations, classes and races;
through the extension of modern science, sanitation,
and machinery to the backward peoples; through the
gradual, peaceful, pervasive influence of the spirit of
universal good-will which they so honestly felt, they
were sure that the benefits of Christian civilization
could be communicated to all the world, within a
measurable length of time, and without serious set-
backs.

It was inevitable that the theology of this era, like its
political credo, should be hopeful, idealistic, easy-

going, world-affirming. In a time when "modern science" and "modern civilization" seemed to be going on from strength to strength, and from triumph to triumph, it was most natural that theology should address to the "modern mind" a plea for reconciliation and partnership; natural that it should find its chief task in keeping up with the rapid intellectual expansion of the era, and believe that all apparent incompatibilities between Christ and Culture should be resolved by the magic formula, "both . . . and." It is ungrateful to speak disparagingly about this type of religious thought, for we still talk and think, in the very act of condemning it, in words and phrases borrowed from the liberal dictionary. Liberal concepts are indeed, for many of us, our whole theological stock-in-trade, and we should be unwise to consign them to the dump-heap until we can get better ones. Yet it is very plain already that they are dead concepts—as dead as the shibboleths of the Gnostics and the Arians, though they have only just died and their flesh is still warm. They have not died as a result of any concerted, effective attack upon their validity, but simply as the result of a general change in the intellectual climate. Their truth and their value will outlive them, of course, as has occurred in the past with other outgrown theological ideas; but it must now be announced, as an accomplished fact, regrettable but duly certified, that their vital sap has departed from them.

The death of liberalism means that multitudes of sincere Christian men, clergy and laity alike, are plunged into a crisis of uncertainty. Liberalism was for many

ministers, as Professor Bennett points out, a "coherent
pattern of theological assumptions"—a "new orthodoxy," which gave self-confidence to their preaching,
and without which they are left with a "feeling of
theological homelessness."[3] How some of these ministers now feel, may be inferred from a letter which I
received in 1933 from a denominational secretary who
had been devoting much of his time to conducting
seminar discussions on the Christian preacher's message for today:

Many of our men are at sea; [he writes] so much so in fact
that too frequently the note of earnestness and conviction,
not to say enthusiasm, is missing in pulpit utterances. For
instance, one of the . . . men called me aside after one of
the seminars and said that for the last two years he had
repeatedly been impelled to call his people together after
church and say to them that they were at liberty to get any
good out of what he had been saying that they found it possible to receive, but that in honesty he wanted to tell them
that he didn't believe it himself. This man was evidently sincere; he represents an extreme type, it is true, but I think our
preachers do need, possibly above everything else, to get their
feet on the ground theologically, or to leave the figure, to
find a new sense of reality in the things they are preaching,
or want to preach.

I venture to suggest that Christian preachers will not
"get their feet on the ground" nor "find a new sense
of reality in the things they are preaching" unless they
can squarely face and clearly come to terms with the
religious requirements of the new era which is upon
us. So long as they attempt to address the men of

[3] *Loc. cit.*

today in the language of yesterday, their words will ring hollow, and they will not even believe their own message, much less inspire faith in their hearers. It therefore becomes the imperative present business of Christian thinkers to turn from the quiet of the library to survey the turbulent spectacle of contemporary affairs; to desert their scholarly preoccupations for the perilous rôle of prophecy; to seek somehow to unravel the plot of the new era in advance, as one deduces the outcome of a mystery story from the—often misleading—clues and hints thrown out in the first chapter.

2. THE RISE OF REALISM

One word alone comes to us clearly, so far, out of the darkness ahead, as a prophecy of the age to come; but in this word, as it seems to me, we have a reliable clue to the whole spirit and temper of the new age. The word is *realism*. Glancing echoes of it are beginning to come to us from many different quarters. *In the realm of politics,* the Fascists and the Communists unite upon at least one point: they regard themselves as true political "realists," and dismiss all moderate or liberal political programs as "unrealistic and romantic." "Unrealistic and romantic"—how often these words are upon the lips of political thinkers like Reinhold Niebuhr, as the shortest formula for pronouncing judgment upon views and policies to which they are opposed! *In the realm of literature,* we are indeed moving away from the more sordid type of realism—sometimes known as naturalism—which prevailed during the Jazz Decade. The "de-bunking" school of biographers and the pornographic school of novelists are beginning to suffer from popular neglect. But, in spite of certain symptoms of romantic nostalgia, there is little prospect of contemporary literature reverting to the style of Emerson and Longfellow. In comparison with such true romantics, contemporary literature remains soberly and faithfully realistic.[4] *In the realm of philosophy,* two earlier movements of thought, known as "Neo-Realism" and "Critical Realism," seem to have little vitality left in them; but a new tide of realism is unmistakably upon us.[5] Whitehead's "provisional realism," first clearly announced in *Science and the Modern World,* has been enormously influential, and, perhaps under his leadership, there is coming to be something like a revival of Platonic and even scholastic realism. It must be confessed that the various forms of realism do not march precisely abreast. Literary realism came upon the scene while political liberalism still lingered, and it may therefore give way to some new literary movement while political realism goes on increasing. Yet all three movements do at least overlap at the present day, and that is enough to

[4] See Oscar Cargill's *American Literature: A Period Anthology,* whose concluding volume, *Contemporary Trends: American Literature Since 1914,* contains a summary of these recent trends by Professor J. H. Nelson. In discussing recent fiction, Nelson concludes that realism, not to say naturalism, "holds its own in America, despite reactions against it, and despite the critical efforts made to discredit the assumptions on which it relies for support" (pp. 9-12).

[5] On the philosophic drift toward realism, see Lyman, *The Meaning and Truth of Religion,* p. 153. For several new varieties of realism, see *Journal of Philosophy,* for March 1, 1934, pp. 113-24, 129, etc.

justify one in characterizing the present as an "age of realism."

Now, it may well be questioned whether the word "realism" can possibly mean one and the same thing in all these different contexts. Between the political realism of Mussolini or Stalin, the literary realism of Zona Gale or Willa Cather, and the philosophical realism of Whitehead or Boodin, there seems to be little enough in common. Yet all these forms of realism have in common a certain temper of mind which craves objectivity and fears subjectivism; which prefers objective realities, however disagreeable, to subjective fancies, however glorious; and which means to be guided by these realities in every form of human quest, whether for truth, or for artistic beauty, or for political stability and progress. We may properly conclude, then, that we are now in the midst of a movement of life and thought as widespread and deep-going as was the romantic movement of the nineteenth century, which expressed itself not only in philosophy and religion, but in literature, the arts, and political affairs as well. As the romantic movement revolted against the rationalism and classicism of the eighteenth century, so we are in revolt—in the name of "realism"—against the romanticism, the idealism, the optimism, the liberalism of the nineteenth century.

If this is a correct account of the temper of our times, it follows that the theology which is needed to give back the "sense of reality" to contemporary preaching will be a *Realistic Theology*. In the general sense above defined, it may be said that contemporary theology has been for some time exhibiting a realistic trend; and many contemporary theologians have already hit upon the word "realism" to describe their position. In Continental Europe, the new theological trend was initiated by the violent revulsion of the "Theology of Crisis" against the subjectivism, the monistic idealism, the world-affirming optimism of Schleiermacher's theology, which has dominated liberal religious thought for over a century. Even the opponents of Barth and Brunner now share to a considerable extent in the same trend toward objectivism, and in the same desire to disentangle Christian thought from its alliance with nineteenth-century secular civilization. Examples of this are to be found in the theology of Georg Wünsch—whose *Wirklichkeitschristentum* might perhaps not inaccurately be translated "Realistic Christianity"—and even in the revised position of Wobbermin, the great defender of Schleiermacher; but the clearest expression of it is to be found in Paul Tillich's book on *The Religious Situation*, where the term "Belief-ful Realism" is used to describe the author's position.[6] In England, theology is much under the influence of the biological realism of Lloyd Morgan and the Platonic realism of men like Archbishop Temple and A. E. Taylor. In America, the objectivistic trend in theology

[6] Cf. Karl Barth, *The Word of God and the Word of Man;* Brunner, *The Theology of Crisis;* Wünsch, *Wirklichkeitschristentum;* Wobbermin, *Zur Überwindung der Gegenwärtigen Krisis;* Tillich, *The Religious Situation,* translated by H. Richard Niebuhr, with introduction by the translator. Adolph Keller, evidently under the influence of Tillich, has adopted the term "Christian realism." See his *Karl Barth and Christian Unity,* p. 299.

began under the leadership of men like Professor Macintosh of Yale and Professor Wieman of Chicago—
convinced empiricists, both, but more interested in the
divine Object of religious experience than in its subjective "feel." In 1931, they collaborated with a large
group of thinkers to produce a symposium called *Religious Realism*. Independently, Reinhold Niebuhr and
others began urging the claims of political realism upon
us.[7] Although there is still a wide distinction between
the various types of theological realism, in Europe and
America, it can fairly be said that they are tending to
converge to form a single movement. It is part of our
present undertaking to make this movement more conscious of its unity, its fundamental principles, and its
peculiar dangers.

I say "its peculiar dangers," for it seems to me that
it would not be wise for us to take up the new shib-
boleth with undiscriminating enthusiasm, join the revolutionary forces with a shout, and fight behind the bar-
ricades of "realism" as if we stood at Armageddon to
do battle for the Lord. We know well, from the history
of thought, what happens at such times as these; how
likely it is that precious values in the older views will
be hastily junked, and have to be salvaged later on with
great difficulty; how likely it is that the new views will
be defined in sharp antithesis to the old, so that they
overleap the truth and fall on the other side. Both
these dangers may be seen in the Theology of Crisis,

[7] Cf. Lloyd Morgan, *Emergent Evolution;* Temple, *Christus Veritas;*
Taylor, *The Faith of a Moralist;* Macintosh, *Religious Realism;* Wie-
man, *The Wrestle of Religion with Truth;* Niebuhr, *Moral Man and
Immoral Society.*

which negates the nineteenth century so vehemently that it practically drives God out of recent history, and opposes liberal theology so antithetically that it manages to be wrong wherever liberal theology is wrong— but in an opposite sense. It is obvious, on the face of it, that realism, unless carefully defined and corrected, involves perils quite as great as those of idealism and romanticism; in particular, the danger of emphasizing the bald and massive aspects of reality at the expense of those invisible capillary forces which do not strike the eye of the average observer, but finally split the hardest rock and the stoutest walls of social captivity and oppression. Surely, the religious thinker must hesitate before whole-heartedly subscribing to the type of literary realism which produced *Main Street* and *Elmer Gantry*, the type of philosophical realism which exalts facts above values, or the type of political realism which rejoices in the death of democracy. *Realpolitik* is an ugly word which will tax all of Reinhold Niebuhr's powers to Christianize! I propose, therefore, that we make it our business, before quitting the camp of liberalism for the camp of realism, to make a fair appraisal of the liberal theology, with a view to carrying over and incorporating into our realistic theology whatever genuine values may be rescued from the wreck, while at the same time candidly recognizing the illusions and shortcomings which have brought the liberal cause to disaster. Since we are especially interested in the immediate future of religious thought in America, our review and appraisal of liberalism may well take the form of an historical analysis of the liberal period in American theology.

3. THE NECESSITY AND ENDURING WORTH OF THE LIBERAL MOVEMENT

In one sense, the liberal movement in American theology may be said to have begun with the arrival of the first settlers. More precisely, it may be dated from the rise of the Deists, the Unitarians, and the Universalists, in the eighteenth century. In a still more restricted sense, it dates back only to the decade between 1840 and 1850, when Theodore Parker and Horace Bushnell began to preach a type of theology as alien to the older Unitarianism as to the older orthodoxy, but deeply akin to the theology of whose passing we are now becoming aware. It is with liberalism in this last and most restricted sense that we are here chiefly concerned; but a word must first be said about the two earlier phases of the liberal movement, which may be called the *Arminian phase* and the *rationalist phase*.

a. *The Arminian Phase*

When a theology emigrates from one cultural habitat to another, something always happens to it. When Calvinism crossed the Atlantic Ocean in the *Mayflower*, it began at once to adapt itself to its new environment, and diverge from the canons of the Synod of Dort in the direction of Arminianism. How could it be otherwise? Calvinism was on the whole—save for all references to the Catholic Church—a faithful reproduction of the theology of St. Augustine, in which the Latin doctrines of the helplessness of man and the sovereign majesty of God had found their ablest and most extreme expression. In the Old World, where medieval feudal civilization still contended with the rising influence of modern commercialism and modern science, Calvinism could rest back for support upon the cultural patterns of the past. Man's humble dependence, for salvation, upon the arbitrary good pleasure of God seemed but the heavenly counterpart of his humble dependence, for the means of subsistence, upon the arbitrary good pleasure of earthly overlords and sovereigns.[8] Even in Europe, these cultural patterns had begun to break down. The rise of the Swiss and Dutch republics and the development of constitutional monarchy in England had done much to cast a shadow of moral doubt upon the notion of an irresponsible divine sovereignty; and already, in free Holland, where the Pilgrims sojourned for a time, they heard echoes of the bold Remonstrance of the Arminians, who sought, so to speak, to impose constitutional limitations upon the sovereign will of God, and regulate the divine Government according to the principles of humane morality. But it was in the New World, where the settlers were free to develop a new type of civilization absolutely unhampered by medieval traditions, that the new political liberalism and the new economic individualism had freest course; and it was inevitable that this should influence theological ideas, even in such tightly ortho-

[8] For some discerning comments concerning the relationship between the Calvinistic theology and medieval cultural patterns, see the "Prelude" of Joseph Haroutunian's *Piety versus Moralism: the Passing of the New England Theology*. New York, Henry Holt, 1932.

dox colonies as those of Puritan New England; for when theological ideas fall out of harmony with political and economic ideas, all the argument in the world will not prevent them from seeming hollow and unreal.

As a matter of fact, we find that the very first generation of Puritan youth born in New England became so far alienated from the Calvinist creed that their parents were forced to resort to that odd measure of compromise known as the "Half-Way Covenant," whereby the children of believers might be admitted to the Communion and so kept within the pale of the Church, although they had never professed repentance or saving faith. A generation later, during the Stuart Restoration (1660-1688), the revulsion against Puritanism in the mother country began to affect the colonies; and from 1720 to 1750 the New England divines were kept constantly busy defending the principles of the Westminster Confession against a mounting tide of Arminian heresy.[9] The more sharply they defined the issues, the more they antagonized the people, it would seem; until at last a new statement of the Calvinist position was made by Jonathan Edwards, which proved able to hold its own for a century.

Jonathan Edwards is generally regarded by liberals as a theological reactionary of the darkest hue, a dour-faced fanatic prepared to assert the most morally repellent doctrines if only he might thereby terrify the indifferent and confound the heretic. He was undoubtedly

[9] Cf. F. H. Foster, *Genetic History of the New England Theology*, p. 7.

set upon defending Calvinism against the assaults of
its antagonists, and was led by his earnestness and his
logic into highly paradoxical positions; but his success
in defending the old creed was due to the fact that he
relived it and rethought it in a highly original fashion.
His was one of the most sensitive, cosmopolitan minds
of the eighteenth century; in remote provincial North-
ampton, and later on in his still more secluded retreat
at Stockbridge, he responded to the main currents of
thought and life that prevailed in his age: the em-
piricism of John Locke, the idealism of Leibnitz, Male-
branche, and Berkeley, the surge of evangelical piety
which simultaneously produced the Wesleyan revival in
Great Britain and the Great Awakening in New England. If the center of the Gospel remained for him
where Calvin had located it (in the sovereignty of
God and the dependence of man), that was because
he had penetrated for himself to the heart of the religious experience of St. Augustine, and come to a mystic vision of all reality and all good as emanating from
God—beside whose Fullness and whose Glory "all
else—earth and self and fellow-men—seemed but 'as
light dust in the balance (which is taken no notice of
by him that weighs), and as nothing and vanity.' "[10]
In his theological works, Calvinism is expounded and
defended with a remorseless logic borrowed from rational philosophy, and at the same time, under the
influence of evangelical piety and Neo-Platonic mys-
ticism, it is inwardly transformed in spirit, so that it
comes to possess something of that strange combination

[10] McGiffert, *Protestant Thought Before Kant*, p. 185.

of mystic sweetness and tragic disillusionment with life that makes the enduring fascination of St. Augustine's *Confessions.*

Edwards's successors were unable to maintain the delicate balance of contrasting interests and elements in his many-sided system; and in their hands the New England Theology became more and more liberal. In spite of Edwards's masterly polemic against the Arminian doctrine of the freedom of the will, there was an unconscious logic in his fervid evangelical piety which could not long be denied. Edwards *preached* as if his hearers had the ability to repent; and he granted them in theory the "natural ability" to respond to the Gospel, while insisting on their "moral inability" to stir an inch out of the bog in which they were stuck, unless predestined and effectually called thereto by irresistible divine grace, which chose whom it pleased and passed by whom it pleased. In the hands of his successors, this purely formal and academic distinction between "natural ability" and "moral inability" grew into an affirmation of genuine free-will, so that Nathaniel Taylor at last could say, "A man not only can if he will, but he can if he won't."

Meanwhile the doctrine of God was undergoing a corresponding modification. Edwards had worked out, in his remarkable *Dissertation on the Nature of True Virtue,* a definition of moral conduct in terms of disinterested benevolence toward "Being in general"; but he had not measured God's conduct by the standard set for man, and had thus exposed his Deity to the charge of callous self-absorption and gross unfairness.

Goaded by the criticisms of the Arminians, who soon found the Achilles' heel of the system, Edwards's successors endeavored vainly to prove that in behaving Calvinistically—predestinating men to sin, and then condemning them to eternal punishment—God was exhibiting disinterested benevolence to Being-in-general. Joseph Bellamy, a pupil of Edwards, maintained that God "*does as he would be done by*, when he punishes sinners to all eternity." Jonathan Edwards, Junior, in discussing the doctrine of the Atonement, provided a rational justification for God's severity by pointing out that, as Moral Governor of the Universe, God cannot be lenient with those who refuse His offer of grace in Christ, without imperilling the general good of the Universe. "God acts," he says, "not from any contracted, selfish motives, but from the most noble benevolence and regard to the public good."[11] In proportion as genuine free-will began to be admitted, these justifications of the character of God began to have some force, for man's damnation began to appear to be his own fault; but the sovereignty of God was to that extent limited, and Calvinism was on the point of passing over into Arminianism.

Thus by a combination of pressures from inside and out—the evangelical spirit bursting out from within and the Arminian moral criticism boring in from without—the New England Theology was at length completely riddled with inconsistencies, and collapsed with a resounding crash. Liberalism had won its first great victory.

[11] Foster, *op. cit.,* p. 203.

b. *The Rationalist Phase*

Long before the collapse of the New England Theology, which may be said to have occurred about the
middle of the nineteenth century—though its ghost
lingered on until after 1880, as the ghost of liberalism is lingering on today—the Arminian phase of the
liberal movement had given way to the rationalist
phase, and the mild, constructive temper of the Angli-
cans and the Methodists had been replaced by the more
corrosive criticism of the Deists, the Unitarians, and
the Universalists. The scope and power of this new
form of liberalism cannot be properly estimated from
denominational statistics. The Unitarians and Universalists have never been very strong, numerically speaking; and the number of genuine Deists in America,
even at the height of the Age of Reason in the late
eighteenth century, was almost infinitesimal; but in
that infinitesimal number three names stand out which
give one immediately a sense of the importance of
the whole rationalist movement: Benjamin Franklin,
Thomas Paine, Thomas Jefferson. Rationalism never
captured more than a small fraction of the American
churches; but it wrote the Declaration of Independence,
inspired the Revolutionary War, and was incorporated
in the Bill of Rights attached to the Constitution. Long
before the Unitarians and Universalists reinforced the
Arminians in their attack upon Calvinism, Americans
had become wedded to a new political morality, which
spoke more of the inalienable rights of man than of the

sovereign will of God, and considered that the chief end of man was *not* the glorification of God, but the pursuit of happiness and the acquisition of property. They were, as Haroutunian aptly puts it, "Calvinists on Sunday and eighteenth century rationalists on week-days."[12]

Of course, it was impossible in the long run to keep the week-day creed from affecting the Sunday creed. Under the Republic, it was more and more difficult to feel the force of a theology which commanded the individual to humble himself and confess his utter depravity before a Deity who resembled George III more than He resembled George Washington. So it was that the years between 1776 and 1840 saw what may not improperly be called an outburst of theological republicanism: the rise of the Universalist and Unitarian churches, and the common assumption, even outside of these churches, that no religious doctrine is acceptable which derogates from the dignity and freedom of man, or the Fatherly benevolence of God. It is not hard to see the connection between these principles and the Universalist creed; it follows directly from the moral worth of man and the moral goodness of God that He cannot permit any human being to perish everlastingly. It is not so easy to see the connection between republicanism and Unitarianism, for the Unitarian controversy early became entangled in speculative issues concerning the person of Christ and the numerical structure of the Godhead, which obscured its main interest. That main

[12] Haroutunian, *op. cit.*, p. 180.

interest was clearly discerned by one of the early critics
of the Unitarian position, Professor Leonard Woods
of Andover:

The religious system set forth . . . in the writings of the
most respectable Unitarians in this country and in Europe,
overlooks *the ruined state of man.* This is the grand, fundamental error of Unitarians. . . . If they should be feelingly
convinced, as I hope through the mercy of God, they will be,
that all men are by nature totally sinful, and totally ruined,
children of wrath, and that God would be perfectly just and
holy should he leave them without exception to perish forever; they would have little difficulty in respect to the other
doctrines which our system contains.[13]

Exactly! But there was just the rub! In our young,
expanding republic, where every man was as good as
any other, it was becoming harder and harder to convince people of the great truth of human depravity, and
get them to admit that a God who let men perish was
just, holy, and worthy of reverence. Most of the orthodox fell back upon the Scriptures as proof of these
doctrines, admitting that they were beyond the purview
of reason. Leonard Woods himself, with what we
should be disposed to regard as commendable realism,
appealed to "observation and experience" as sufficient
grounds for belief in human depravity; but observation
and experience seemed to his contemporaries to point
all the other way, as we may gather from the following
declaration by his Unitarian antagonist, Professor Ware
of Harvard:

[13] Leonard Woods, *Works,* Vol. IV, pp. 338-339. Quoted in
Haroutunian, *op. cit.,* p. 215.

Innocence, and simplicity, and purity, are the characteristics of early life. Truth is natural; falsehood is artificial. Veracity, kindness, good will flow from the natural feelings. . . . I insist, that if we take a fair and full view, we shall find that wickedness, far from being the prevailing part of human character, makes but an inconsiderable part of it.[14]

I have dwelt particularly upon this feature of the rationalist credo because it was just this *optimism about man and God* that outlived the rationalist movement, and became part of all modern liberalism, down to the year 1914. When Theodore Parker and Horace Bushnell began to preach their new liberalism, based upon German philosophical idealism, shortly before the middle of the nineteenth century, they questioned most of the basic assumptions of their predecessors, but they never questioned the assumption that *whatever is best, is, or is to be.* Optimism had by this time become a part of the American disposition, an ingrained conviction which financial panic, civil war, and political corruption could not disturb for long. As John Bennett says, "The premise of Liberalism is faith in man and his highest values as the clue to the nature of God."[15] This premise was first clearly enunciated by the Universalists and Unitarians, but later became the common property of all theological "progressives." Whatever its inadequacies, it has at least purged our theology of much that was morally shocking and rationally incongruous.

[14] Ware, *Letters addressed to Trinitarians and Calvinists,* pp. 24-26. Quoted in Haroutunian, p. 212.
[15] *Loc. cit.*

c. *The Great Age of Liberalism* (1849-1914)

But it would be misleading to suggest that the theology of Parker and Bushnell was in any deep-going sense continuous with the older rationalism. It was so new, that the history of American theology might well be split in two at the point where their influence began to be felt—just as the history of German theology is split in two by the advent of Kant and Schleiermacher. With Parker and Bushnell, in fact, there came into American theology that self-same distrust of abstract reason, that self-same trust in moral faith and religious intuition which had worked such a revolution in German theology a half-century earlier. The provincialism of the American mind had kept it apart from these powerful currents of thought for all that time; but now, through channels that are not hard to trace, they began to penetrate with revolutionary force. Parker went directly to the fountainhead, and read German theology in the original. Bushnell came in touch with German thought indirectly, through Coleridge's *Aids to Reflection*—the book to which British and American religious liberalism owes more than to any other single writing. The philosophy which the great Unitarian and the great Congregationalist derived from these sources was substantially the same: an idealistic monism which broke down the old barriers between reason and revelation, natural and supernatural, secular and sacred, and found God immanent in all things. It was the same philosophy; but Parker preached it polemically, while with Bushnell it became a means of conciliation and reconstruction. He is the Schleiermacher of American liberalism, as Parker—with his three great "instinctive intuitions," God, the moral law, and immortality—is in a sense its Kant. Parker did more than Bushnell to break down the old dualistic theology, based upon miracle, prophecy, and supernatural revelation. Bushnell did more than Parker to create a new theology in which the timeless truths of Christian experience were reclothed in the thought-forms of the nineteenth century. It is to Bushnell, then, that we must go for the classic formulation of this "New Theology," as we must go to Jonathan Edwards for the classic formulation of the "Old Theology" which it replaced.

Bushnell's two basic concepts are those which underlie all forms of romanticism: (1) the superiority of intuition to reason, and (2) the world as a developing organism, whose indwelling spirit is God.

The first of these two concepts is best enunciated in the *Essay on Language*, which may be regarded as the indispensable preface to all Bushnell's works. This essay is an eloquent protest against the "stern, iron-limbed speculative logic of our New England theology,"[16] both orthodox and Unitarian, which takes itself so seriously only because it fails to perceive that words and logical concepts, in the religious sphere, have a merely symbolic, analogical truth, mixed with inevitable error, which grows worse and worse in proportion to the length of the chain of reasoning based upon them. The true basis of theology is not to be

[16] Bushnell, *God in Christ*, p. 96. New York, Scribner, Armstrong and Co., 1877.

found by torturing the words of Scripture, but in a *"Perceptive Power* in spiritual life . . . an immediate experimental knowledge of God"[17] which expresses itself more fitly in the language of poetry and paradox than in logical concatenations of ideas. The theology which would spring from such a method would not be based on any rigid creed, it would be able to embrace many creeds simultaneously, as moments in a complex truth, essentially inexpressible. It would be less clear and precise than the old theology, because it would spring from "a humbler, and far less positive state of mind,"[18] and would recognize the human and subjective elements in all deep religious convictions. The essential mood and temper of liberalism were never more accurately expressed than by Bushnell in this essay. Its irenic spirit, its vagueness of language, its disparagement of theological system and clear thinking, its capacity to embrace mutually contradictory propositions with equal affection, are here set forth with disarming frankness.

The second of Bushnell's basic concepts appears in all his chief works, but most plainly in *Nature and the Supernatural*. The fundamental proposition of this book is the fundamental proposition of post-Kantian idealism: that *man* belongs to the supernatural realm (or as the philosophers would prefer to say, the supersensible world) as truly as God belongs to it. Man is superior to nature because he possesses personality, which comes not under the law of cause and effect but

[17] *Ibid.*, p. 93.
[18] *Ibid.*, p. 94.

under the moral law. If, then, man is incomprehensible from a purely naturalistic standpoint, it is fair to assume that the divine personality will express itself in many miraculous acts incomprehensible to man; and yet the acts of God will, from the divine point of view, be perfectly lawful. Nature and the Supernatural together constitute one great organic whole, one "system of God," all governed by the divine purpose, all revealing the divine presence in various degrees. In *Christian Nurture*, Bushnell had already applied this concept of universal divine immanence to *the family*, and had argued that the child growing up in a Christian home might be ingrafted into the life of God through becoming an organic participant in the life of the family, by a simple developmental process, without the need of any extraordinary and unnatural crisis of conversion. In his work on *The Vicarious Sacrifice*, he argued that the atoning work of God in Christ was to be seen in the vicarious suffering that is inherent in all true love, so that atonement is a part of every Christian's duty, and operates yesterday, today, and forever. All life, indeed, and all the universe become from this point of view revelations of the immanent God, and the absolute distinctions of orthodoxy, between natural and revealed theology, between other men and Christ, are transformed into relative distinctions of degree and not of kind. If Bushnell speaks, in a famous chapter, of "The Character of Jesus forbidding his possible classification with men," it should be noted that it is Christ's *character* rather than his wondrous works that so distinguishes him; and Bushnell demands of every Christian that he should be a "Christed man," reflecting the Master's character so far as in him lies.[19]

The theology of Bushnell is essentially identical with that liberal theology which is passing away before our eyes. In making this statement I am fully conscious of the fact that new and powerful influences have molded the liberal mind since Bushnell's day. Evolutionary natural science, Biblical criticism, and the new social conscience are the three most important of these modifying factors. But the remarkable thing is, that all three of these influences, challenging and disturbing as they were when they first appeared, proved amenable to interpretation in terms of Bushnell's ideology. *Nature and the Supernatural* had nothing in it which was in the least inconsistent with the acceptance of Darwinian evolution, or any other scientific theory, unless one were to interpret these theories as implying—what certainly could not be proved—that the world of naturalistic cause-and-effect, as scientifically analyzed and described, was the whole real world. *The Essay on Language* made it possible, in principle, to accept quite calmly all the most radical results of Biblical criticism, since it made plain the distinction between the eternal ideas of the Bible, which must always be grasped by intuition and experience, and its temporary thought-forms and modes of expression, of whose secondary and

[19] For an excellent brief analysis of Bushnell's contribution to American theology, see John Wright Buckham's book, *Progressive Religious Thought in America*, pp. 6-32. I am indebted to this book for a general perspective upon the whole course of American liberalism, although it confines its attention almost exclusively to the Congregational Church.

transient character Bushnell was convinced long before it was proved by the critics. Finally, in his *Christian Nurture* and other practical writings, Bushnell had already transcended the individualistic psychology and ethics of the rationalistic school, and arrived at a view of the social dependence and social responsibility of the individual, quite consonant with the views arrived at much later by social psychologists and social reformers. None of his basic concepts had to be unlearned or discarded; they had only to be expanded to cover new accessions of knowledge and to express new social aspirations. In 1914 as truly as in 1849, when Bushnell's first important writing, *God in Christ,* was published, the one great idea of an immanent God, whose presence may be intuitively apprehended throughout the length and breadth of nature and in all the institutions of civilized society, proved adequate to express the whole Gospel and solve all theological problems. The *Ultimate Conceptions of Faith* which George A. Gordon expounded, in one of the greatest theological writings of the twentieth century, are all in substantial harmony with Bushnell's faith.

American theology in this respect followed a course more nearly parallel to British[20] than to German theology. The modern liberal movement in theology inaugurated by Schleiermacher at the beginning of the nineteenth century did not enjoy an undisputed sway throughout the rest of that century in the land of its

[20] On the general trend of British theology during this "immanentist" period, see C. C. J. Webb, *Religious Thought in England from 1850.*

origin. After a period of mounting prestige that carried it—with the aid of Hegel and his school—well past the middle of the century, it met with a sharp reaction, and gave way to a rival liberal school, the Ritschlian, whose cautious scientific temper and ethical emphasis were more akin to the humanitarianism of the eighteenth century or the "positivism" of Auguste Comte than to the mystic piety and romantic idealism of Schleiermacher. Oddly enough, the influence of Schleiermacher and Hegel upon British and American religious thought began to be operative just about the time that their influence began to wane in Germany; and the influence of Ritschl, instead of being *subsequent* to that of Schleiermacher and Hegel, was *simultaneous* with it. The result was important: the two schools of German theology *neutralized each other* in the British and American mind, and left as their residual deposit a very moderate and tolerant type of liberalism, in which the mystical emphasis of Schleiermacher and the ethical emphasis of Ritschl were both to be found, side by side.

A good example of this will be found in the theology of my honored predecessor in the chair of theology at Oberlin, President Henry Churchill King. Like most American theologians of his generation, King had studied in Germany and fallen under the spell of the reigning Ritschlian school, as represented by Wilhelm Herrmann; but at the same time he was influenced by the idealistic philosophy of Lotze, which continued the Schleiermacher-Hegel tradition in the latter part of the nineteenth century. These two contrasting influ-

ences, neutralizing and supplementing each other, gave
to King's thought a kind of rich texture, combined with
a sobriety and moderation which disarmed criticism
and commanded respect. His well-known book, *Reconstruction in Theology*, still remains the best analysis
of the forces which combined to produce the latest
form of the liberal theology; and his statement of that
theology remains one of the sanest and most persuasive.
In a way, the work of King may be taken as the *terminus ad quem* of the great age of liberalism, as that of
Bushnell represents its *terminus a quo*.[21] The two positions are not identical, but are in essential harmony—
as may easily be seen by comparing King's treatment
of the question of miracle with Bushnell's. The idea
of *continuity*, of the unity of all things in God, runs
through this whole movement of thought from Bushnell to King—as the idea of *discontinuity* runs through
the thought of Karl Barth, its great antagonist. In my
opinion, we cannot afford to abandon this central idea
of liberalism, however we may be forced to qualify it.[22]

[21] It may be questioned whether the work of William Adams Brown
does not represent a more fitting terminus for the liberal movement;
but the striking characteristic of Dr. Brown, in my estimation, is his
command of the whole history of Christian thought, which in a way
lifts him out of his own period in history, and gives a kind of
catholic and timeless quality to his thought.

[22] For a judicious summary of the enduring truths in the liberal or
"immanentist" theology, see the conclusion of Professor C. C. J.
Webb's *Religious Thought in England from 1850*. Cf. The conclusion of Buckham's *Progressive Religious Thought in America*. Cf.
also the previously cited article of John Bennett, "After Liberalism—
What?" For the most incisive criticism of liberalism, the reader must
be referred to an article on "Modern Liberalism" by a great Unitarian
thinker, the late Dean Fenn of Harvard Divinity School, published
in 1913 in *The American Journal of Theology* (Vol. 17, pp. 509-519).

If an unqualified emphasis upon unity, organism, continuity lands us in a sort of pantheism, an unqualified revolt against it may land us in an equally disastrous deism, in which all sense of God's presence as an operative principle in the world may be lost.

4. HUMANISM, BARTHIANISM, AND REALISM

Not all American theology of recent date has maintained King's even-handed balance between the philosophic, scientific, religious, and ethical interests; nor has the influence of the two rival schools of German theology always been so completely united. Some of our religious thinkers, like Lyman Abbott in his *Theology of an Evolutionist*, have been mainly concerned to recast Christian theology so as to bring it into harmony with natural science; others, like William Newton Clarke and Harry Emerson Fosdick, have made it their life work to adjust theology to the new view of the Bible; others, like Walter Rauschenbusch, have been exclusively concerned to make of theology a proper vehicle for the "Social Gospel." As a rule, these diverse interests have been unified by the common acceptance of an idealistic world-view like Bushnell's; indeed, it may fairly be claimed that idealism was the reigning American philosophy throughout the first decade of the twentieth century, and Josiah Royce was our leading philosopher. But in that same decade there occurred a sharp revolt against idealism, led by the two great pragmatists, William James and John Dewey, and seconded after a time by another rebellious group calling themselves the "New Realists." The realist revolt had at the time no visible effect upon theology; but the pragmatist revolt found an almost immediate response in the "Chicago school," which was already committed to a kind of left-wing Ritschlianism, strongly scientific, critical, and practical in temper. Under the leadership of Shailer Mathews, Ames, Beckwith, and G. B. Smith, Chicago had been moving after John Dewey in the direction of a social, pragmatic, humanitarian form of Christianity, long before the name "humanism" was applied to the more extreme forms of this tendency.[23]

Even before the World War, then, we may note certain signs of internal disintegration in the liberal theology, presaging its present decline and fall. The remarkable thing is, not that it finally fell, but that it lasted as long as it did. It was not built tightly and firmly on the "logic is logic" principle, like the "one-horse shay" of Oliver Wendell Holmes' poetic parable, which fitly symbolizes the New England Theology; it was sketchily designed and loosely built, and its parts were of unequal strength and worth. If, therefore, it continued to serve as a sufficient vehicle for American religious thought down almost to the present day, that was mainly because American life continued calm and prosperous so long after other countries were storm-ridden. Swept with a hurricane of desolation and despair, before which no flimsy fair-weather vehicle could stand, Germany abandoned the liberal theology soon after the war. Karl Barth became to her the prophet

---

[23] On the humanist movement, see my *Theism and the Modern Mood,* Chapters I and II. I shall not repeat here that description and criticism of humanism, which I still think substantially correct.

of a new Gospel, in which stern world-denial sup-
planted the complacent world-affirmation of the nineteenth century; and his grim message has received a
sympathetic hearing in all the Protestant countries of
Europe. It has been received as a righteous judgment
upon liberal Christianity even by those who could not
accept its constructive theories.

Adolf Keller has shown how, wherever the Barthian
teaching has gone, discussion has passed through three
stages. In the first, the sole effort is to *understand* the
new theology objectively; in the second, a heated discussion arises (mostly hostile) as to its merits and
dangers; in the third, a mood of humility falls upon
the critics, and they recognize that here is a movement
of thought which cannot be answered with arguments
and accusations, but only through a thoroughgoing
self-examination and a complete reconstruction of life
and thought.[24] American theology, aware from the start
of the Barthian movement, has lingered in the first of
these three stages long after other countries have entered the third; but now, under stress of suffering, the
American mind is beginning to feel the force of Barthianism for the first time, and react to it with some
heat. In this fact I find one more decisive indication
that the liberal period in American theology is ended,
and a new epoch has begun.

I cannot believe that, for us in America, the teaching of Karl Barth points the way out of the present
theological dilemma. Negatively, as a criticism of the
liberal theology, we shall do well to lay it to heart;

[24] Keller, *Karl Barth and Christian Unity*, pp. 31-34.

but positively, it cannot help us to a new statement of the Gospel, and that for a simple reason: we have just recently abandoned Calvinism, and cannot be expected to enter with any sense of joy and emancipation into a movement whose slogan is "Back to Calvin." Doubtless we are now in a position to appreciate better than our immediate predecessors the "realistic" element in Calvinism: its willingness to face the harsh and tragic side of life quite candidly, and scale down its hope of salvation to the very modest dimensions which are sufficient to take in the small number of mortals who give any plausible indication of having received divine election. Yet we cannot so soon forget the awful dilemma in which our grandfathers were caught, in the declining phase of the New England Theology; and we know that our fathers, when faced with the choice of accepting Calvinistic tradition or venturing out along untried paths, found themselves pretty generally in Dr. Fosdick's position: "With me," he once said, "it was not a question of New Theology or Old Theology; it was New Theology or No Theology." I believe that American theology has much to learn from Barth and his disciples, especially from his more moderate interpreters such as Emil Brunner and John McConnachie; but if Count Keyserling is right in saying that Barth's teaching presents the one way of salvation for modern Protestantism, then many of us must be content to be numbered among the lost. To us, Barthianism seems as wide of the mark on one side as humanism is on the other; it is an unstable combination of a crude realism with respect to man and a wistful idealism with respect to ultimate reality, just as humanism is an unstable combination of a crude realism with respect to ultimate reality and a wistful idealism with respect to man. For us, then, it is once more a case of "New Theology or No Theology"; and so far as we can now see into the future, the only New Theology that gives promise of being adequate to the stresses and strains of the new era is a *Realistic Theology*.

It will be our task in the succeeding chapters of this book to restate some of the chief Christian doctrines from a realistic point of view. In thus applying realistic principles to theology, we shall be explaining the meaning of realism far better than it possibly could be explained in any preliminary definition. Realism is in fact hardly more than a temper or attitude at present, and it will have to be defined bit by bit, coöperatively, as various theological pioneers set out from different points, blazing trails through the realistic wilderness. For myself, I can say only this much at present: that the word "realism" suggests to me, above all, a resolute determination to face all the facts of life candidly, beginning preferably with the most stubborn, perplexing, and disheartening ones, so that any lingering romantic illusions may be dispelled at the start; and then, *through* these stubborn facts and not *in spite* of them, to pierce as deep as one may into the solid structure of objective reality, until one finds whatever ground of courage, hope, and faith is *actually* there, independent of human preferences and desires, and so casts anchor in that ground.

Realism, so conceived, is bound to follow a different

method from that which idealistic thought has followed, ever since Kant. It will beware of the method of postulation with its insistence that God must be precisely such an One as our human moral standards demand for their support. It will hesitate to assume, before proof, that "the real is the rational and the rational the real," as Hegel claimed. It will begin by looking out at the external world, not inward at the realm of mind. It is prepared to accept a God who is a "consuming fire" and a terrible Judge, as well as a loving Father, and it is willing to recognize chaotic, tragic, uncontrollable, and even devilish factors in reality, if candid observation leads to such conclusions. Obviously, a realism of this sort is not at war with all that liberalism has stood for. The love of truth, the appeal to experience, the readiness to accept new knowledge from any well-attested source, were elements of enduring strength in liberalism. In so far as liberalism possessed a genuinely scientific spirit, willing, as Huxley said, to sit down before the facts humbly, like a little child, it was already realistic. Its romantic illusions began when it assumed that scientific correctness and philosophical breadth in a theology were enough to give it saving power. In its eagerness to correct the Bible in the light of modern science, it rationalized away some of the deepest Christian truths. It was politically inept, sociologically shallow, psychologically stupid when it supposed that humanity could be delivered from its ills by sweetness and light, by gentle permeative influences, instead of by convulsions and bloody sweat. With the collapse of our utopian ideals in the World War, and the passing of middle-class prosperity in the great depression, we are beginning to perceive that our human predicament is far more serious than the nineteenth century ever imagined, and that science is not an adequate Messiah to lead us out of it. To the realistic analysis of that predicament we turn in our next chapter.

Chapter II

A REALISTIC VIEW OF OUR
HUMAN PREDICAMENT

THAT the human race is caught in a serious predicament of some sort is the common assumption of all religious systems and all working philosophies of life. We shall probably not be guilty of unrealistic thinking if we start with the conviction that this common assumption is true. The very existence of religious plans of salvation and philosophic ways of life proves that the course of human existence does not and never did run smooth. So much travail of mind and soul never would have been wrung from man—who after all does not rack his brain or discipline his desires unless somehow driven to it—if it were not true that something is seriously wrong with our human condition, and threatens to become worse unless we can cure it or make our escape from it or find protection against it.

If religions and philosophies are at one in this common assumption of a human predicament, they differ radically in their theories as to where the key to this predicament is to be sought. Indeed, it might be claimed that the question on which religions and philosophies divide most decisively and fundamentally is the question, "What is the root of all evil?" or otherwise stated, "With what deep-lying sources of frustration and disappointment have we human beings most seriously to reckon, if we would attain the greatest good and avoid the greatest ill?" Here, then, is an appropriate starting point for our realistic reconstruction of theology—doubly appropriate because it is so characteristic of realism to begin by facing the worst.

To *begin* by facing the worst. I do not mean to say that realism and pessimism are synonymous, although that is undoubtedly the popular impression of the matter. To luxuriate in gloom is just as characteristic of certain romanticists who inherit their addiction to melancholy from Schopenhauer or Edgar Allan Poe, as it is characteristic of realists of the Theodore Dreiser variety. A healthy-minded religious realism is no more committed to coarse, muck-raking cynicism than it is committed to the neurotic nightmares which darken the minds of romantic melancholiacs. Religious realism is not—as has so unjustly been said of Reinhold Niebuhr's realism—a form of defeatism. It seeks a sure ground of hope, a Gospel for the poor in spirit, as earnestly as any other school of religious thought. But it is determined not to be taken in by idealistic illusions, as was the generation which fought the "war to end war"; and to puncture all such illusions at the start, it likes to begin by surveying all the difficulties and obstacles that stand in the way of man's salvation. In this, the realists resemble old-fashioned orthodox Christians more than they resemble the liberals of yesterday.

This last statement will presently be sustained by a comparison of the traditional Christian view of our human predicament with that of the liberals; but first of all, let us consider certain pre-Christian views, that we may understand why Christianity, when it came, was welcomed as "good tidings of great joy" by a weary and disheartened world.

1. PRE-CHRISTIAN VIEWS

When our remote ancestors first became humanly conscious, and took note of themselves and their environment, they must simultaneously have become conscious of trouble and danger as deeply interfused elements in the whole human situation. For them, the root of evil naturally was found, in the main, in the external world, where hostile powers of all sorts seemed to be lying in wait for the unwary man, to do him harm. Fierce wild beasts, human enemies, scorching drought and raging storm, insect plagues, and insidious diseases, the recurrent perils of night and winter, the precariousness of food and shelter and the constant danger of accident in a world little understood: these were the chief ills which our ancestors had to guard against.

But we shall have little conception of their plight if we view their environment through our own eyes, matter-of-factly and scientifically. Nothing was matter-of-fact in that world; everything was the product of mysterious powers—ghosts, demons, nature-spirits, or plain undifferentiated wonder-working force (*mana*) —and in the midst of this terrifying cloud of unseen witnesses you had to walk very circumspectly, indeed, if you were to avoid the various ill-omened acts for which you might be struck dead. Luck was king in that confused world; magic art and religious ceremonial aimed at propitiating King Luck, and making it possible to secure a modest living on his domains; but he was an arbitrary despot, and might strike at you unexpectedly, for no reason at all, no matter how carefully you observed the taboos, and no matter how many amulets you wore. A terrifying predicament, indeed, bad enough in fact and made doubly bad by fear-struck imagination! If primitive animism were religion's last word, then it might seem necessary to conclude, with Lucretius and Karl Marx, that religion itself was a large part of the "root of evil," and salvation would largely consist in getting rid of it! Better no religion at all, one sometimes feels, than such a religion of terror.

A great clarification and simplification of the whole human predicament took place when religion conceived the momentous idea that the world is not a world of Luck, nor a world, so to speak, of Pull, where one may get what one wants by wheedling and bribing the ruling powers, but a world of Moral Law, playing no favorites, and rewarding or punishing each act with precisely the consequence which it merits. John Oman, in his book *The Natural and the Supernatural*, has a remarkable passage on this conception of "action and award" as the ancient analogue of the modern conception of "cause and effect."[1] It had its great vogue, as he points out, in the sixth century B.C.—when it appeared simultaneously in India, Persia, Palestine, and Greece—and it had a creative influence upon the practical arts and upon jurisprudence, parallel to the influ-

---

[1] Oman, *The Natural and the Supernatural*, pp. 218-230. New York, Macmillan, 1931.

ence of the concept of cause and effect upon technical progress in the nineteenth century A.D. In India, it was called Karma; in Greece, Nemesis; in Persia and Palestine, it was identified with the righteous Will of God. It goes without saying that the human predicament becomes enormously more hopeful when the world thus takes shape as an ordered moral universe; for the root of evil is no longer found in external, uncontrollable forces, but is brought within man's grasp. Immoral conduct, rebellion against divine law, is now the root of evil; for in its simplest form the new creed affirms that the righteous man invariably prospers, while the unrighteous invariably meets with misfortune. In such a world one can walk with a firm tread and an undistracted mind, looking only to the moral law for guidance and trusting in personal merit or integrity as the key to all life's problems.

Unfortunately, experience does not confirm the truth of this principle in its simplest form. Within the bounds of earthly life, moral rectitude is not closely correlated with prosperity, and moral obliquity is often scandalously successful. To argue that great sufferers must necessarily have committed great sins, in strict proportion to the degree of their misery, is to flout and pervert that very moral sense on which the whole theory rests for support—as Job's comforters abundantly illustrate. Unless, therefore, the concept of "action and award" can be corrected, it affords no adequate diagnosis of the human predicament, and may actually deepen the burdensomeness and distress of life. On the whole, it may be said that in India and Greece the correction of the concept led toward apathy and despair, while in Persia and Palestine it led toward energy and hope; for in the first-named countries the injustices of the present life were explained by referring them to a former state of existence or to some fixed principle, while in the last-named countries they were explained as temporary injustices, to be rectified at some future date.

I do not mean to suggest that Indian Karma and Greek Nemesis were wholly false and misleading concepts, nor that Persian dualism and Hebrew Messianism were free from fanatical and harmful illusions. But it must be admitted that when the idea of transmigration is united with the idea of Karma, to form the notion of an endless "wheel of rebirth," at each stage of which a man's lot in life is precisely determined by his conduct in a previous existence, the result is deadening in the extreme. As soon as this notion became fixed in the Indian mind, the human predicament became practically hopeless, and the sole way out of it was to escape from life altogether, into some passionless pool of peace above the realm of time and change. In Buddhism, this pessimistic diagnosis of the human predicament found its most completely logical expression in the theory that the root of all evil is desire, which is itself the root of all individual existence. In so far as undisciplined desire and passionate attachment to transient things are really basic factors in our human predicament—as I believe they are—Buddhism must be regarded as one of the keenest diagnoses ever made of the whole human problem; but if there is any real, enduring worth in that individual existence which the average man struggles so feverishly to preserve, and if the frustrations of life come in part—as we now know they do—from preventable natural calamities and social injustices peculiar to particular types of society, then it is too simple a diagnosis to find the root of all evil in desire; and to cure the ills of life by curing the desire to live is like curing a headache by decapitation.

I am aware that the Buddhist Nirvana does not necessarily mean extinction, and that in certain forms of Mahayana Buddhism an eternal value is ascribed to individual life; but the fact remains that, throughout the ancient East, wherever the Indian idea of Karma still holds sway, and Western ideas have not come in to break the spell, a fatalistic apathy weighs down upon the souls of the people, and makes them accept social evils like caste or banditry and natural calamities like flood or pestilence, with the same hopeless shrug of resignation. "My Karma is bad"—that is the one unfailing diagnosis which explains, and perpetuates, all the ills of life. Once more, religion seems to have created evils greater than those it tried to diagnose and cure, and made our human predicament worse instead of better.

The predicament of the Greco-Roman world in the time of Christ was strikingly like that in which India and the Orient have found themselves since the law of Karma was first formulated, and in which they would apparently always have remained if outside influences had not come in to disturb their trance-like immobility. The belief in a "wheel of rebirth" played no such rôle among the Greeks and Romans as among the Hindus and Buddhists, although Plato himself had believed in it; but the idea of an endlessly revolving wheel of eternal recurrence, resistlessly urging on all lives, all civilizations, all worlds, to their own ultimate destruction, was accepted as basic. The perfect symbol of human life was the circling of the heavens; for human destiny was believed to be determined by the motion of the stars, and whenever, at the end of the Great Cycle, all the planets came round again to the same positions, affairs on earth would be found to be exactly what they had been at the corresponding point in all previous cycles. According to the Stoics, the whole universe was destined to be dissolved, once in every Great Cycle, into the Divine Fire from which it came, and when it came forth once more after the conflagration it would be precisely what it was before, in every detail. Time and history meant nothing in such a world; earthly events were moving toward an ignominious end —moving irresistibly, impelled by a Necessity and Destiny beyond human control, to which even the gods were subject.

The root of evil, under these circumstances, was bound to be located just where India had found it, in the one region still left, as the Stoics said, "in our power": the human heart, with its inordinate attachment to the things that pass. The only escape from this predicament was through the same ancient way that India had found: calm acquiescence in the evils of this mortal life, detachment from all passionate ambitions and fears, aspiration toward and eventual union with the Eternal One that abides in the midst of change.

Between Buddhist extinction of desire and Stoic apathy, Hindu absorption in Brahman and Neo-Platonic absorption in the mystic One, there is little to choose. To the Western activist, tired with hustle and bustle and disappointed about the outcome of some short cut to the millennium, these ancient religions and philosophies have all the charm of a long-forgotten half-truth. There are few of us who would not gain in poise and serenity from a reverent and meditative reading of the *Discourses* of Epictetus or the *Dialogues* of Plato, or still better—*experto credite*—by spending a day or two in a Buddhist monastery in some quiet mountain retreat in Japan. So long as the race shall last, however we may progress in our conquest of the powers of nature and the injustices of the social order, an important part of the human problem will consist in the disciplining of our wayward desires and the achievement of an attitude of resignation toward the inevitable limitations of finite existence; and so long will the pre-Christian sages have much to teach us. Yet when all this has been said, it must be regretfully recorded that these sages left the human race in a pretty hopeless plight. They not only failed to get to the bottom of our human predicament; they wove about it a web of theory which concealed the real facts and discouraged further analysis. Not without reason, perhaps, did Dante consign the pagan philosophers to a region which, while devoid of the tortures of the infernal depths, nevertheless lay beyond the portal marked with the inscription "Abandon *hope*, all ye that enter here."

2. ORTHODOX AND LIBERAL CHRISTIAN VIEWS

Christianity, when it began to spread among the disinherited classes in the metropolitan centers of the Roman Empire, was welcomed as "Good News." How could it be otherwise? Hitherto, the earthly life had possessed no great worth, and future history held nothing to which to look forward. The philosophic ideal, high and hard to achieve, was to live one's life as an harmonious part of the Stoic World-Soul or the Neo-Platonic One, and fly off after death to the region beyond the moon, where time and change were no more, and where mortal spirit merged with immortal Spirit like a bubble of air escaping from the depths of a slimy pool to rejoin its proper element. That ideal was not for the many but for the few. The multitudes were more drawn to the various Oriental religions which were pushing in at this time to supplement the dying religion of the Olympian gods. Among these Oriental redemptive religions Christianity was at first inconspicuous; but it rapidly forged to the front, for it clothed individual life with unique significance, and it invested the future with an incomparable radiance. It was significant that the only serious rivals of Christianity, Mithraism and Manichæism, both hailed from Persia; for Persia alone in the ancient world possessed a religious tradition which rivaled that of Palestine in the significance it gave to the time-process. The idea of a cosmic struggle between Light and Darkness, in which men might participate on the side of the Light and so help turn the tide of the universe toward truth and righteousness, gave real dignity to individual life and real dramatic significance to the course of history. It may help, therefore, to bring out the depth of the Christian message if we compare its view of the human predicament with that of its Persian rivals, and speculate upon the reasons for its triumph.

Christianity agreed with the Persian cults in what may be called the "fighting-chance" theory of our human predicament. Instead of regarding the natural and social orders as fatally fixed and hopelessly beyond repair, as Indian and Hellenistic thought tended to do, Christian and Persian thought saw the whole creation as the scene of a mighty conflict between good and evil, a conflict whose present drift was dark and dubious, but whose ultimate outcome was to be, if not the abolition of evil, at least its subjugation. On one side in this mighty struggle were arrayed the righteous, under the leadership of the most high God, and a host of heavenly angels; on the other side were arrayed the wicked, under the leadership of the Adversary (Satan or Ahriman) and all his mighty demons: "for we wrestle not against flesh and blood, but against principalities, against powers, against the rulers of the darkness of this world, against wicked spirits in heavenly places."[2] For Greek and Indian thought, all time and change were ultimately meaningless, and hope must soar vertically upward toward the unchanging and immovable; for Persian and Christian thought, the eternal issues were being fought out here and now in the temporal

[2] Eph. 6: 12. Last five words retranslated to clarify the meaning.

world, and hope looked forward as well as upward—
upward for God's help, forward to the day of victory.

This "fighting-chance" theory had in it, as we can
now plainly see, many survivals of animism, and many
features in common with the "Karma" theory of the
human predicament; but it differed from raw animism
in having its good and evil spirits organized into two
regular standing armies, fighting according to the rules
of civilized warfare instead of prowling and pouncing
upon poor mortals unpredictably and irresponsibly like
ghostly guerrillas; and it differed from the "Karma"
theory in that it did not furnish a deadening moral
justification for the *status quo*, but looked forward with
a kind of revolutionary ardor to a "new heaven and a
new earth." It located the source of evil partly in man
and partly beyond him, and in so doing made it impossible for man to escape from it alone. That, by itself, made this view of the human predicament pretty
discouraging; but if man allied himself with the celes-
tial powers of good, the new view offered him a chance
of participating in a real victory over evil, far different
from the "sour grapes" sort of victory which was the
best the pagan sages could offer. To destroy or subdue
wild powers, natural and social, to secure concrete bless-
ings here and hereafter, was very different from learning
not to have any wants, and to accept ills as if they were
goods.

So far, the Persian and Christian views were at one,
and had the same advantage over their common rivals.
They differed mainly in what might be called *historical
concreteness*. The Persian cults began and ended in an

atmosphere of mythology. They dealt with the supposed exploits of the sun-god Mithra or the "primal man" or the "æons of light." Christianity, on the other hand, inherited the Hebrew conception that history was punctuated with a series of "mighty acts" of God, who had intervened in the course of events repeatedly, at different times and places, to "put down the mighty from their seats, and exalt the humble and meek." This He had done, according to the Hebrew view, in fulfillment of His part in a solemn covenant made first with Abraham and then renewed through Moses; so that wrongdoing, from the Hebrew point of view, took on the form of a willful breach of contract, an act of rebellious ingratitude toward a covenant-keeping God. In Christianity, this feeling of the "sinfulness of sin" was still further deepened through the belief in a culminating "mighty act" whereby God himself had, so to speak, entered the human drama as a participant. In Christ, it was believed, God had shown His love for erring humanity by sending One who was no mere mouthpiece or ambassador, but his "only-begotten Son"; and at a given place and time, outside the walls of Jerusalem, at a place called Golgotha, when Pontius Pilate was procurator of Judea, God had permitted His Son to be cruelly done to death by those he came to save. Sin, for the Christian, thenceforth became something worse than a breach of contract; it was a denial, a betrayal, a re-crucifixion of one who "loved us and gave himself for us." Neither Mithraism nor Manichæism could point to God's presence in history in any such concrete and dramatic sense.

Here it was that the prophet Mani made his great mistake. By announcing himself as successor to Abraham and all the true prophets, Mani clothed his message with something of the definite concreteness of the Hebrew sacred story, as Mohammed did later; but while he gave to "Jesus" a place among his forerunners, he regarded him in Gnostic fashion as a heavenly æon of light, too pure to become incarnate in human flesh, too divine to suffer or to die. This phantom Jesus, who never stooped to suffer, had no such power to inspire repentance or command loyalty as had the real Jesus, born of a humble Jewish maiden, cradled in a manger, trained in a carpenter's shop, doer of gracious deeds, friend of sinners, nailed on a cross between two thieves, laid in a tomb, triumphant over death and sin for our sakes. Herein lay the superiority of the Christian view of the world-struggle: it made the struggle seem real, by correlating it with actual recent events and persons, while the Persian cults still left the contending hosts of good and evil wrapped in the same mist of unreality which enshrouded the figures of the dying Olympian gods. *Christianity triumphed, because it took evil more realistically than any other religion, and presented a hope that was invincible because it grew out of the heart of the starkest tragedy.*

It is not easy to summarize the orthodox Christian view of our human predicament, since it has varied considerably in the course of the centuries; yet it can be said without fear of contradiction that orthodox Christianity finds the root of all evil in *sin*. The world as it came from God's hand was good; wicked angels and wicked men have spoiled it. Greek Christianity emphasized the fleshly corruption, the mortality, the blind ignorance which have resulted from sin, and prescribed severe ascetic-mystic discipline as part of the cure. Latin Christianity emphasized the guilt of sin, the legal liability to eternal punishment in hell to which it exposed us all, and prescribed obedient performance of penance as the chief means of cure. Orthodox Protestantism painted the predicament of sinful man—his darkened mind, his totally perverted will—in such lurid colors that it appeared man could do nothing by himself to get out of it, and must cast himself wholly upon the mercy of God. All forms of orthodoxy agree, however, in regarding sin as something more than a momentary misdemeanor, committed by an individual; it is a collective disease with which all humanity is afflicted, and with which every individual is infected from the moment of his birth, or rather from the moment of his conception. This disease did not originate with man; it was caught by the first man from one of the fallen angels, whose sin consisted in the fact that they had preferred to live for themselves, when they might have chosen to live only for God. Fallen mankind, together with the fallen angels, forms a vast mass of corruption and perdition that darkens heaven and earth, and will inevitably be consigned to hell in the final great setting-to-rights, unless God's grace intervenes to create a fundamental change of nature in each heart. Beside this colossal evil, all bodily hardships, all social maladjustments, and death itself seem minor evils easily to be borne. Let the sinful human heart be changed, and all other evils will take care of themselves; so long as it remains unchanged, all attempts at external reform are bound to fail.

I believe that orthodox Christianity represents a profound insight into the whole human predicament. I believe that the basic human difficulty *is* that perversion of the will, that betrayal of divine trust, which is called sin; and I believe that sin *is* in a sense a racial disease, transmissible from generation to generation. In affirming these things, the Christian Fathers and the Protestant Reformers spoke as realists, and could have assembled masses of empirical evidence to support their views. Of this, more presently. Meanwhile, we must grant that at two crucial points their diagnosis failed to do justice to the human situation: (1) it laid such stress upon sin in general, as a universal human condition, that it failed to grapple realistically with the causes of particular sins; and (2) it failed to recognize that among the things "necessary for salvation" are some means of overcoming the niggardliness of nature, so as to produce food enough for all, and a just organization of society to secure the equitable distribution of natural and human gods. Failing adequately to realize the importance of these problems, the medieval Church attempted to stifle the spirit of free investigation when it began to be interested in natural and social science; and the modern era began with a great revolt against ecclesiastical authority. The dream which animated the new secularistic society was the Baconian dream of endless material progress through scientific discovery and invention. It is the chief distinguishing

characteristic of liberal Christianity that it has adopted
the Baconian dream as part of the Christian hope, and
thus come to regard ignorance instead of sin as the
root of all evil.

It would be ungracious to minimize the enormous
success of the scientific, cause-and-effect approach to
reality, or to deny the essential soundness of its diagnosis of one fundamentally important side of our
human predicament, the problem of overcoming the
niggardliness of nature. Under scientific analysis, man's
natural environment has been shown to be, not nig-
gardly at all, but bounteous beyond all the wildest hopes
and dreams of our pre-scientific ancestors, an inex-
haustible treasury of riches which man may have for
his own if he will but faithfully trace out and follow
the cause-and-effect relationships which are the key to
the treasury. Not only has science solved for us, in
principle, the basic problem of a sufficient food-supply
for all the inhabitants of this planet for an indefinite
time to come, it has performed unlooked-for miracles
besides: put powers into our hands that rival the thun-
derbolts of Jove; filled our households with conven-
iences and comforts that set us free, if we will, for the
cultivation of the life of the spirit; waged successful
war upon pestilences which used to be accepted humbly
as divine punishment; and by improved means of trans-
portation and communication, overcome a large part
of those finite limitations of space and time which used
to distinguish the life of man from the life of the
immortal gods! Small wonder that Man the Omnipotent, the Omnipresent, the Omniscient, should begin

to fancy himself in the rôle of Supreme Deity, erecting skyscraping temples to himself, and dreaming stupendous, grandiose dreams of the splendor of his future achievements! Through modern man, it began to appear, the Universe first had become conscious of herself, and begun to act as if she knew what she was about! If ignorance was the root of all evil, creative intelligence knew how to tear evil up by the root; and the services of ancient sages and saviors were no longer required. Professor Montague has fitly expressed this scientific faith and hope in a great passage of his book called *Belief Unbound*:

Neither Gautama, with his sympathy for all life, nor Jesus, with his flaming compassion for humanity, could realize the possibility of mastering the world without either abandoning or destroying it. The forces of evil were great and dark, and the power of secular intelligence was hardly visible. To Buddha, all individual life is poisoned at the source, and existence itself must be abandoned. For Jesus and his disciples the situation is less hopeless. Life itself could be saved and personality enhanced and perfected, but only by the destruction of this world and the creation of another. There was infinite courage, but it was the courage of despair, the strange flutelike courage of the weak in body to face death when exalted by spirit and its unearthly vision. But they did not know, and could not know, the kind of courage that has come to us, unworthy though we be, through science. Ours is the easy courage born of confidence and well-grounded hope. It is the reasoned faith that we can use the world if we cannot conquer it, and by harnessing the forces of nature to the demands of intelligence, transform an ancient foe into a patient friend and ally.

Enthusiasm must then, for any modern mind and in any

truly modern ethics, include, along with the old-time courage of the heart, the new courage of the mind, the resoluteness to use intelligence to the limit in all dealings with our physical environment, our social institutions, and our own inmost selves.[3]

These words of Professor Montague, written in 1930, reflect the belief which still lingered on during the administration of Herbert Hoover, that the removal of our social and personal ills was simply an engineering proposition, in the same category with flood control or improved communications. Given the truth of that conception, the conclusion inevitably follows that with the application of scientific intelligence to our human as well as to our physical problems, a society without poverty, without inequality, and without serious distress of any kind is already in sight, and we have already entered upon the home-stretch that leads to Utopia. That being granted, Professor Montague very properly goes on to consider the difficulties which old-fashioned religion will encounter in a world free from evil, and decides that the only sort of religion which will henceforth satisfy the intelligent man is one which promises to crown all the satisfactions which he can secure by his own powers with a supreme superhuman satisfaction: the consciousness of being at one with the Infinite.

In making this suggestion, that religion must now prepare for Utopia by ceasing its aggressive warfare against evil and becoming a joyous quest for positive values, Professor Montague follows a line of thought

[3] W. P. Montague, *Belief Unbound*, p. 60. New Haven, Yale University Press, 1930. Quoted by permission.

very characteristic of liberal Protestantism.[4] Professor
Machen in his well-known diatribe, *Christianity and
Liberalism,* draws a telling caricature of the typical
liberal parson assuring his self-satisfied flock that although they are very good people, very good indeed,
he knows of something that will make them even
better! Now if we are really on the road to Utopia, and
know how to master all our ills by science, without the
aid of religion, Professor Machen's taunts are ill-timed;
but in the light of recent events, one is bound to admit
that Montague's liberalism now seems more antiquated
than Machen's fundamentalism. It is very evident today
that science alone is not going to bring in the social
millennium and that the creation of ideal human relationships is a different problem from the mastery of
nature.[5]

It is significant that our most accomplished and
prolific designer of Utopias, Mr. H. G. Wells, has
given us in his 1933 model, *The Shape of Things to
Come,* a far more serious picture of our human predicament than he has ever drawn before. The sufferings and disappointments of the Great War have long
since borne fruit in Mr. Wells's thought; and in more

[4] Troeltsch in his *Glaubenslehre* mentions it as one of the distinguishing marks of the modern mind that it replaces the sense of
sin with the urge toward fullness of life.

[5] In the Church of St. Gervais in Paris, where a Big Bertha shell
came through the roof in the midst of a Good Friday service during
the war, I once heard a priest discussing the theory of "salvation by
science." At a dramatic climax in his discourse he suddenly pointed
to the vault above, where the marks of the explosion were still
plainly visible, and exclaimed, *"La science, la science,—voilà ce
qu'a fait la science!"*

than one of his recent writings[6] he has recognized the
need of a deep-going religious discipline of life to prepare the social reformer for the sufferings he must
endure; but nowhere has he so exposed the tragic
frustrations of our times as in this prophetic panorama
of the near future.

Hope springs eternal in the Victorian breast, and in
his last chapters Mr. Wells gives us a prospectus of
future earthly bliss in his best 1895 manner. Complete
human solidarity having been achieved by the year
2059, and the last vestiges of national antagonism having vanished in the World Commonwealth, the scientific leaders of mankind set to work to "key up the
planet," and achieve marvelous results: free production of new species of plants and animals, eugenic
control of human evolution, "geogonic planning" to improve climate by elevating mountain ranges, moral education so successful that all governmental restraints
can be removed, collective ownership so nicely organized that one can travel about without luggage, claim-
ing free food and lodging and free supplies for every
need wherever one goes. All this, that is to happen a
hundred years hence, is in the most approved style of
scientific utopianism.

But between us and that blissful Elysium rolls a dark
Acheron of calamity, described in a very different vein:
a breakdown of finance and of social morale, a great
wave of crime and brigandage, destructive wars in the
Far East and in Europe, frightful outbursts of hatred

[6] For example, in his brilliant sketch of an evolving World Commonwealth in *The Open Conspiracy.*

and intolerance, a general decline in public health and standards of living, leading at last to a pestilence that sweeps away half the population of the globe and makes it possible for a few well-organized aviators to establish a World Dictatorship. Throughout this terrible narrative, the thing that seems to haunt Mr. Wells's mind, as an inexplicable enigma, is the fact that, when the road to Utopia is so plain to the mind, the human race somehow is paralyzed or bewitched, and cannot reach out its hands to take what is so plainly within its grasp. *It cannot will its own plain good.*

What to Mr. Wells is a dark enigma, and to most liberals a source of profound disillusionment, is nothing strange or unduly disturbing to orthodox Christians. They know of old this spell of enchantment that binds man's will and makes him unable, like a man in a nightmare, to reach out and actually touch that good which reason shows him is within his grasp. It is the ancient "mystery of iniquity," described by St. Paul in his *Epistles*, and by St. Augustine in his *Confessions*. To orthodoxy it is plain that unless the grace of God shall attack and cure this disease of sin, neither science nor any other form of human effort will ever get man over the Acheron of calamity into Mr. Wells's Elysium. No mere hundred years will transport us across that yawning chasm, for it is the chasm between hell and heaven, sin and grace, which only God can span. Without power from on high, man must stand forever paralyzed and entranced on this side of the gulf, stretching out helpless hands toward the vision that forever eludes him.

I do not wish to bring unjust accusations against liberal Christianity. It cannot be simply identified with the Religion of Science. It has never asserted that man can be saved by science alone, and it has had almost as much to say about sin (at least in its textbooks of theology) as has orthodox Christianity itself. But consider what its response would have been, if the question had been put to it sharply, "Why, having at last by grace of science enough to eat on this planet, can we not divide it fairly and live in peace and harmony together? Why can we not live the perfect Christian life now, both individually and collectively?" I doubt very much whether liberal Christianity would have answered, bluntly and decisively, "Because we are sinners." It would have said something about sin, to be sure, but it would have meant the sort of thing that can be expected to yield to improved methods of religious education, not something that infects the whole life of the race;[7] and it would have had quite as much to say about "the need of understanding."

Understanding—that was the great word of the liberal era! How often it was used, at hands-across-the-sea banquets, at missionary board meetings, at summer conferences on social service, at rallies in the interest of International Conciliation! If only there could be "better understanding" between Labor and Capital, Immigrants and 100 per cent Americans, Orient and

---

[7] This criticism does not apply to the "Social Gospel" school of liberalism, whose position will be considered later.

Occident, Negroes and Whites, all would be well! In other words, if the same critical analysis were applied to social problems that has been applied to the forces of nature, the great and essential step toward their solution would have been taken. Now it would be quite perverse to claim that the intellectual understanding of social problems was impossible or valueless; it is, on the contrary, an indispensable condition for effective social action, which has in the past been too much neglected; but the more persistently we apply scientific analysis to our whole human predicament, the more surely shall we discover that it contains stubborn factors which do not automatically disappear before the light of "understanding." Among these stubborn factors is one that corresponds closely to what Christian orthodoxy has called sin.

3. CHRISTIAN ORTHODOXY AND MARXIAN COMMUNISM

We have seen reason, then, to prefer the more traditional Christian account of our human predicament to the more modern, as in many respects the more realistic and free from illusions. But this does not mean adherence to it in all its details, nor does it eliminate the possibility that some alternative diagnosis of the human problem may call attention to important factors which Christianity has overlooked. Among the alternative diagnoses which our sick world is getting today from a multitude of physicians, the most influential and important is that of Marxian communism. It differs so sharply from that of Christianity, and challenges its accuracy so aggressively, that no contemporary Christian thinker can afford to ignore it. Let us endeavor, then, to come to grips with the Marxian position by comparing its view of our human predicament with that of Christian orthodoxy, and coming to our own conclusions upon the issues at stake between them.

According to Karl Marx and his disciples, the crux of the whole human problem lies in the field of economics. The religions, the philosophies, the moral codes, the political struggles, the characteristic manner of life of each distinct form of society are determined, in the words of Friedrich Engels, by "the prevailing mode of economic production and exchange, and the social organization necessarily following from it."[8] Trace the history of man's way of making a living, noting the close connection between "production-mode" and social structure, and you will have the key to the whole history of his quest for the good life.

The story begins idyllically, with "primitive tribal society, holding land in common ownership."[9] The break-up of this primitive communism brings the serpent of individualism or private property into the collectivistic Eden: and society splits up into competing classes, each having its characteristic outlook on life determined by its special economic interests, and each striving to subdue or exploit the others through securing a dominant influence in the political State. So long as the tools of trade continue to be of such a nature that each man can possess his own, private property continues to belong, in the main, to the individual who

[8] Preface to the *Communist Manifesto*. Chicago, Kerr, 1915.
[9] Engels, *loc. cit.*

produced it. But with the advent of large-scale machine production in the late eighteenth and early nineteenth centuries, it is no longer possible for the worker to own his own tools. Property and political power thus inevitably fall into the hands of the capitalistic or machine-owning class, which uses its advantage to defraud the workers of a large part of the product of their labor. Competitive at first, capitalistic society becomes increasingly monopolistic, the number of the possessors diminishing and the number of the dispossessed continually increasing. This inevitably leads at last to its downfall, since the decline in domestic purchasing power drives capitalistic governments into imperialistic competition for foreign markets, and this leads to terrific wars—whose chaos gives the disinherited proletariat its opportunity to arise and "expropriate the expropriators." The few who *have* are unable any longer to control the many who *have not*. Thus is inaugurated—after a brief "dictatorship of the proletariat"—a truly classless society, which resembles capitalistic society in its highly scientific and technical modes of production, but resembles primitive communism in its collective ownership and collective control of the processes of distribution.

This impressive construction of universal history is phrased by Marx in philosophical terms, as well as in economic. Philosophically, the three epochs of Primitive Communism, Historical Society, and Higher Communism correspond to the three stages of Hegel's dialectic: thesis, antithesis, and synthesis. Theologically, they seem to bear a close resemblance to the primitive *status integritatis*, before the Fall, the historical *status corruptionis*, in which we are now living, and the final consummation to which we look forward, in the orthodox Christian scheme of history.

In spite of these formal resemblances to Hegelian and Christian thought, the Marxian theory really is "something new under the sun," and presents a view of our human predicament which had never been seriously considered before. As against the regular Hegelian view, that the continuity of history is to be found in the rational sequence of its governing ideas, Marx contends that the continuity of history is to be found, so to speak, in the history of the *tools* by which man has earned his living, and "ideologies" are merely the rational arguments and slogans by which men have defended and pursued their economic interests. As against the orthodox Christian view, that man's fall is due to sin and his redemption is possible only by divine grace, Marx contends that man's fall is due to the institution of private property, which itself is due to a change in his manner of making a living, and man's redemption will be accomplished by the inevitable working of economic forces. This contrast is perhaps too absolute, as just stated, for Christianity has often contended that "the love of money is the root of all evil," and Karl Marx denounces the evils of the capitalistic system as if they were in some sense sinful, or at least cruelly unjust. Communistic hatred of the capitalist is unreasonable if the capitalist is merely the victim of the system, and not in some degree its responsible organizer and eager defender. Yet in general the distinction holds good that the communist locates the root of evil in the economic system, while the orthodox Christian locates it in the corrupted will of the responsible individual.

Reinhold Niebuhr tells an anecdote that brings out clearly the practical consequences of the orthodox Christian view of sin. A bishop of the Russian Orthodox Church was recently on a visit to America, where he was sharply questioned by a group of czarist sympathizers who suspected him of Communistic leanings. One asked if he prayed for the soul of the Czar; another asked if he prayed for Stalin. "Yes," answered the bishop, "I pray for the soul of the Czar and for Stalin and for every sinner including myself." And he made it plain to his auditors that he was absolutely indifferent to governments and social orders, provided that he was permitted to continue what to him was the one great task of the Christian Church: the saving of sinners.[10] This attitude is characteristic of Christian orthodoxy, both Catholic and Protestant.

I can distinctly remember my own first reaction to the crisis of the World War, which came at a time when I was most completely under the dominance of the evangelical type of Protestantism. It seemed to me that wars, revolutions, and efforts at social reconstruction were simply irrelevant phenomena from the Christian point of view, except as they led men to realize their sinfulness and seek salvation. A life devoted to the construction or defense of a social system was a life wasted, so far as I could then see; for all social

[10] Niebuhr, *Reflections on the End of an Era*, pp. 223, 224.

systems were ephemeral houses of cards, destined to swift collapse because of the flimsiness of the human materials of which they were built. If one wanted to improve human life, let him devote himself to the Gospel ministry, in the evangelical sense: a ministry of regeneration, whereby *human nature*, otherwise unchangeably corrupt, might be transformed by supernatural power, and so afford materials for a better world.

I am not altogether ashamed of having taken this stand, for I still believe that it represents a profounder diagnosis of the human problem than many Utopian schemes of social reform. Even from the social point of view, the results of individual "life-changing" may be far-reaching, as appears, for example, in the fresh attack upon the race problem which has arisen from the Oxford Group Movement in South Africa.[11] Yet it is easy to see how such an attitude blinds one to the positive truth in the Marxian diagnosis of our human predicament, and how inevitable it was that communism should take a hostile attitude toward Christian orthodoxy, for this reason alone, quite apart from its historical connection with the czaristic system.

What, then, shall be our attitude in the presence of this sharply-drawn issue between Christian orthodoxy and Marxian communism? Is it true that "you cannot change human nature," apart from supernatural grace? Is the religious transformation of the individual the key to all possible social improvement, or is the trans-

[11] See the April, 1930, *Letter* on *The South African Adventure*, published by "The Group."

formation of the economic order the key to the transformation of men's lives? Is the root of all evil to be
found in sin, or in economic maladjustment, or in some
more comprehensive term? As the results of the Russian
experiment come to be more fairly and accurately as-
sessed, we shall be able to give more precise answers
to these difficult and important questions. Already,
however, two conclusions seem to emerge with some
distinctness: (1) human nature is by no means so
rigidly fixed as orthodoxy has supposed; and (2)
human failings and miseries of many sorts remain to
be dealt with, after economic maladjustments have been
removed.

As to the first of these two points, I should consider
that such books as Ella Winter's *Red Virtue* and Harry
Ward's *In Place of Profit* were decisive. Before such
evidence as they present, the orthodox (and capitalistic) contention that the natural man will not work
unless spurred by the hope of private profit has simply
been annihilated. It has been found possible in the
Soviet Union to change men's moral attitudes profoundly by altering the economic and political system—
so profoundly that one wonders uneasily, after reading
such books as Miss Winter's, just how the two species
of humanity which live inside and outside Russia are
going to be able to talk intelligently with one another!
At the same time it is evident that many of the fundamental human drives, for recognition, sexual com-
panionship, and the like, have remained relatively constant in the new social context; and this leads to our
second contention, that even the complete solution of

the economic problem is not automatically going to clear up all human ills. Egotism remains a persistent human trait in the Soviet Union; only, as a clever contributor to the *Atlantic Monthly* remarks, it takes the typically communistic form of "wangling" privileges from the bureaucracy instead of the typically capitalistic form of beating some other individual in a "horse-trade."[12] Our recent experience, during the economic boom, should convince us that general economic prosperity does not inevitably make for complete human blessedness. Russia herself, when the economic struggle eases up a bit, is likely to find herself in the midst of a "Jazz Age" which will convince the more sincere devotees of communism that individual self-discipline is an important part of the human problem.

The evidence would seem to point, then, not to the abandonment of the concept of sin, but to its realistic definition and expansion in a Marxian direction, including in it henceforth those economic and social ills which Marxianism so emphasizes. Fortunately for us, this task of reinterpreting the concept of sin has already been begun and more than half completed by that significant type of liberalism known as the "Social Gospel" movement. In its earlier phases, the movement shared in many of the "illusions of liberalism," and expected the triumph of the "kingdom of God on earth" to come too swiftly and easily, by the peaceful penetrating influence of a "spirit of good-will and

[12] "Wangling versus Horse-Trading," *Atlantic Monthly,* November 1933 (Vol. 152, No. 5, pp. 635-637. Anonymous article in the "Contributors' Club").

friendly understanding." But in Walter Rauschenbusch, its greatest prophet, it found an exponent whose grasp of economic and sociological processes was profoundly realistic. If in the early years of his career he permitted himself to hope too lightly, his last great work, *A Theology for the Social Gospel,* was written amid the chaos and heartbreak of the World War, and belongs in many respects to the New Era.

As against the common liberal belief in the goodness of human nature, Rauschenbusch boldly defends the belief in original sin. Even in the *biological* sense, he points out, it is true that the race is one, and evils like feeble-mindedness are transmitted from generation to generation. Still more truly is the race one in sin through *social heredity*, which transmits corrupt practices and attitudes continually from the old to the young, from social institutions to their members. This is more than the "force of example," to which Pelagius appealed; sin draws its power to seduce the individual "from the authority of the social group in justifying, urging, and idealizing wrong, and from the decisive influence of economic profit in the defence and propagation of evil."[13] Rauschenbusch's conception of original sin heads up in the conception, already suggested by Schleiermacher, Ritschl, and Josiah Royce, that when social institutions go wrong, they become "super-personal forces of evil," whose sinister power, perpetuated from age to age, links all times and places at last to-

[13] Rauschenbusch, *A Theology for the Social Gospel,* p. 67. For a similar view, based upon a social psychology, see Coe, *Social Theory of Religious Education,* chapter on "Sin."

gether in one great "Kingdom of Evil," the Satanic counterpart of the Kingdom of God.

In some of our swampy forests [he writes] the growth of ages has produced impenetrable thickets of trees and undergrowth, woven together by creepers, and inhabited by things that creep and fly. Every season sends forth new growth under the urge of life, but always developing from the old growth and its seeds, and still perpetuating the same rank mass of life.

The life of humanity is infinitely interwoven, always renewing itself, yet always perpetuating what has been. The evils of one generation are caused by the wrongs of the generations that preceded, and will in turn condition the sufferings and temptations of those who come after. . . . The Mexican peon is ridden by the Spanish past. Capitalistic Europe has fastened its yoke upon Africa. . . . When once the common land of a nation, and its mines and waters, have become the private property of a privileged band, nothing short of a social earthquake can pry them from their right of collecting private taxes.[14]

Rauschenbusch's conception of original sin seems to me to constitute a middle term which makes it possible to unite the Marxian and orthodox Christian diagnoses of the problem of evil in one unified view.

Marx's claim that practically all historical States have been governed in the selfish interest of a ruling class, is fully granted by Rauschenbusch. Not only imperial Germany but so-called democracies as well, he boldly asserts—and it took considerable boldness to say this in 1917, are in reality governed by parasitical groups. He would probably have agreed that there is a sense

[14] From Rauschenbusch, *A Theology for the Social Gospel*, pp. 78, 79. New York, Macmillan, 1917. Quoted by permission.

in which every political State is the product of original sin, since its very constitution is principally shaped by a powerful group which seizes the lion's share of the privileges, and seeks to secure them to its heirs and assigns in perpetuity. Had he read Mr. James Truslow Adams's *Epic of America*, he would have seen in it much to confirm this opinion. For the rank and file, even in this land of "equal opportunity" and "the American dream," the only way to claim their heritage in hard times was to go to the frontier and wrest it from the wilderness and the Indians.

But there is a sense of conscience in Rauschenbusch which differentiates him from Marx, and allies him with orthodox Christianity. There is not only a sense of anger at the privileged, there is a sense of sharing in their guilt, a sense of contrition, that is profoundly Christian and profoundly un-Marxian. And this is most just; for who of us is so devoid of privilege that he does not in some sense participate in ill-gotten gains? Every American participates in the ill-gotten gains of the Mexican War; every white man profits by the age-long exploitation of the Negro; and in so far as he does not in some way discharge his debt to these defrauded groups—as Albert Schweitzer did by going to Africa as a doctor—he shares in the *guilt* of his father's sins. So to view the matter is to be as realistic as Marx, and as conscious of the guilt of sin as St. Augustine— nay, more conscious, for it is impossible to feel as guilty about Adam's Fall as one may rightly feel about more recent and definite wrongdoing. No one individual can be held responsible for any great social wrong; it roots in an objective, impersonal social structure which is largely the product of economic causes, as Marx pointed out. But no individual can wholly escape responsibility for the persistence and extension of such a social structure, in his own time. Hence it is proper to refer to it as social *sin*, and not simply as social *maladjustment*.

4. THE THREE MAJOR FACTORS IN OUR HUMAN PREDICAMENT

I think it has become evident, in the course of our survey of conflicting views, that there are three major factors in our human predicament, none of which can safely be overlooked in any comprehensive philosophy of life: *the individual, the social, and the cosmic,* or, if you please, *the enemy within, the enemy around, and the enemy beyond.*

In our dealings with the *cosmic* order, we are in a predicament because of our *finitude* and our *ignorance*. Science has done much to reduce our finitude and increase our power over nature, but until it can abolish earthquakes and tornadoes, old age, sickness, and death, man will remain little and helpless in the presence of nature, and a degree of *resignation* will still be required of him, like that which the Ancient East has practiced to excess.

In our dealings with the *social* order, we are in a predicament because of the *self-reproducing power of unjust institutions*. There was a time when the wars and depressions which spring periodically from social injustice were taken as incomprehensible "scourges of

God," in the same class with the Black Death and the seven-year locusts. A sensitive conscience can still discern in them a form of divine punishment; but their causes are now seen to be of so general a nature that individuals and small groups are almost helpless in their presence, and the responsibility for their occurrence cannot possibly be pinned upon a few diplomats or a few bankers. Karl Marx is right: the economic system is determining our social structure, which in turn is producing our wars and depressions, with mechanical inevitability. The progress of technical invention is now beyond any man's control; and with each new invention is initiated a chain of consequences which no man can fully foresee. Social science is not enough, religious devotion and altruistic good-will are not enough to extricate us from this predicament. What is required, in order to carry us over into the ideal society of which we dream, is an actual transfer of power, property and privilege; and thus far in history no great mass of men has consented to such a transfer except under duress.[15] In the heat of war, in the depths of a

---

[15] As an outstanding exception to this principle, the voluntary relinquishment of their feudal rights and privileges by the Shogun and the chief nobles in Japan, at the time of the restoration of the power of the Mikado, is often cited. (For instance, in Shailer Mathews' *Spiritual Interpretation of History*, p. 185.) I would not minimize the patriotic motives of these feudal lords, nor would I deny that their voluntary action made possible both a more peaceful and a more radical shift in national policy than could have occurred if they had been less unselfish. But I remember the words of a well-informed Japanese friend, to whom I once extolled the Shogun as a model of self-abnegation: "You must not forget that the nobles were bankrupt, and the new government took from them the burden of their debts." Actually, this episode is an excellent illustration both of the working of politico-economic pressure, and of the way in which graceful yielding to such pressure may avert bloodshed and disaster.

depression, men feel their common kinship and promise heroic sacrifices; in drawing up the peace treaty or in emerging from the depression, the selfishness of group interest reasserts itself, and we are back in the old predicament. O wretched men that we are! Who shall deliver us from the body of this death?[16]

Finally, in our dealings with *ourselves*, we are in a predicament because of that weakness, division, and perversion of the will, that preference of the lesser to the greater good which theology calls *sin*. Ignorance and stress of circumstance play their part in the wrecking of personality; social institutions seduce and pervert their members in innumerable ways; but unless the central core of personality has been destroyed altogether, the man who has done wrong and been detected will still stand up and acknowledge, "I did it. I take responsibility for it. I might have done otherwise, though strongly tempted. I am not wholly to blame, but I will bear my share of the guilt." Perhaps man's dignity never stands forth more grandly than when he makes such an acknowledgment. The pity of it is that the power of self-direction thus confessed is so

---

On the causes of the bankruptcy of the Japanese nobles, see Sansom, G. B., *Japan: a Short Cultural History*, pp. 454-62, 505-17.

[16] Would Reinhold Niebuhr be prepared to respond antiphonally at this point, "I thank God through the class war and the uprising of the disinherited!" Perhaps not. Would Harry Ward? Perhaps. Personally, I should regard the class war, real as it is, *not* as a way out of our social predicament, but as a part of the predicament from which we need to be delivered. Grinding poverty, bitter resentment, desperate insurrection do not prepare the proletarian mind for scientific diagnosis of social ills nor for even-handed justice in administering the remedy. When social protest boils up from below, and triumphs through violent revolution, it tends to create a new disinherited class which must revolt in its turn—and so on *ad infinitum*.

little developed and so poorly used; that the forgetfulness induced by routine and the alluring charms of lesser goods are perpetually detaching the will from that perfectly possible Better and supremely worthful Best whose reality it recognizes in the very act of self-condemnation.

Thus in all three realms it appears that man is in a predicament from which there is no simple or easy way of escape. Science is valuable to him in all three realms, especially in the realm of nature; but even there it cannot rescue him from his finitude. Political action is important for him, especially in the social realm, whence its effects spread out into the individual realm; but what man is wise enough to devise and execute the perfect political program, which will infallibly lead to individual well-being and social justice? Religion is indispensable to him, above all in the realm of the inner life, whence its influence spreads out in concentric circles into wider and wider realms; but what man can create the perfect religion?

If man is ever to be saved from his ills, it is well that he should begin by facing the seriousness of his predicament, as we have endeavored to do in the present chapter. This done, he must next face the question whether he is alone in his efforts to find a way out, or whether his feeble intelligence and hesitating will can depend upon the operation of deep and powerful forces which make for his deliverance; whether he must dig his own way out of his prison unaided, or whether there is a Friend on the outside. That is the question of the Providence of God, to which we turn in our next chapter.

CHAPTER III

A REALISTIC FAITH IN THE PROVIDENCE OF GOD

I. PROTESTANTISM AND PROVIDENCE

CARDINAL NEWMAN once said that the only doctrine in which Protestants believed with all their hearts was the doctrine of Providence. One need not subscribe to the implication that Protestants have only one sincere belief, but one must surely acknowledge that Newman had a shrewd eye for the real center of gravity in the Protestant faith. Down to the present generation, for conservative and liberal Protestants alike, the doctrine of Providence has been the living center from which all their warmest convictions have sprung, and to which they have retreated as to a citadel when their more secondary and peripheral beliefs have been threatened.

It is not hard to see why this was so, in the case of the Protestant Reformers. They were in rebellion against the authoritative institution which had guided and controlled the affairs of Western Europe for over a millennium. Outside of that institution, it was claimed, one could no more be saved than outside the Ark of Noah in the time of the Flood. Well, they were outside, and very conscious of their exposed position. They had certain temporal princes as their allies; and the heathen Turks quite unintentionally helped them out from time to time by making forays into Catholic Europe; but humanly speaking their position was precarious if not desperate. "Did we in our own strength confide, Our striving would be losing." One thing alone supported their courage: the conviction that the Providence of God was on their side, and whether living or dying, they were safe under His almighty protection. So they could confidently sing,

> And though this world, with devils filled,
>   Should threaten to undo us,
> We will not fear, for God hath willed
>   His truth to triumph through us.

The Reformers' faith in Providence was a *fighting* faith; that is what we must bear clearly in mind if we are to understand the lengths to which they went in asserting it. It did for them what certain forms of fatalism have always done for soldiers and men of action. The soldier who believes that he will not be hit except by the one shell that "has his number on it," or that he will not die until the day that is "set," acquires thereby a self-possessed coolness and indifference to danger. So it was with Luther, Zwingli, and Calvin; they believed that God foreknew and foreordained everything that was to come to pass in the whole history of the world, and no one could snatch out of His hand the soul He had determined to save.

They always denied that this doctrine was fatalistic, and endeavored in many ways to distinguish their belief in Providence from the Stoic belief in Fate as well as from the Epicurean belief in Fortune. Nothing is merely fortuitous in this world, they contended, and nothing is determined by any merely natural cause-and-effect Necessity or Fate, since nature and man alike are subject to the Sovereign Will of God. They rescued this teaching from the quietistic consequences of some forms of fatalism by insisting that one of the decrees of Providence is that we should in many matters provide for ourselves. "He . . . has also made us provident of danger," says Calvin, "and, that they might not oppress us unawares, has furnished us with cautions and with remedies."[1] If this doctrine sometimes seemed to make men helpless puppets of God, and so humble them in the dust, its actual effect was usually to exalt and energize them; for were they not instruments in the hand of God, for showing forth His glory and defending His Kingdom against the craft of the Sons of Belial?

Nevertheless, it must be said that many of the difficulties of fatalism recur in the Reformation doctrine of Providence. Luther denies the freedom of the will in opposition to Erasmus, so vehemently as to imperil the sense of moral responsibility. Zwingli asserts that God's Will is the only real Cause, and thus makes God the author of evil. Calvin asserts that God predestinated Adam's fall, and the damnation of all but the elect, for reasons that it is impious to investigate. The only way to rescue God's goodness, after this, is to maintain with the Stoics that partial evil is universal good, or with the Arminians that God's decrees in relation to the wicked are merely "permissive." But the Reformers in general were so intent upon asserting the omnipotence of their divine Protector that they scorned to

---

[1] *Institutes,* i.17.4. The whole of this chapter (17) is a valiant attempt to escape from fatalism.

mitigate the logical consequences of their faith. They believed in the goodness of God, as well as in His power; but if compelled to defend it they sometimes answered tartly, with Zwingli, that He who made the laws of the universe was above the laws which He made.

For moral inconsistencies of this sort the theology of the Reformation was condemned at last to destruction. The remarkable thing is, that when liberal Protestantism attacked the older theology, in its Calvinistic form, it left the doctrine of Providence still standing, and continued to regard it as the core of the Christian faith. Providence and Predestination were so closely connected in Calvinism that it would seem hard to attack the latter without impugning the former; and yet Theodore Parker, the severest of all the liberal critics of Calvinism, clung to the doctrine of Providence as if it were the Rock of Ages. It is easy to understand why he did so, and why many other liberals did the same. Having given up the belief in God's extraordinary and miraculous intervention in human affairs, he laid all the more stress upon God's regular and orderly government. This, in fact, with the belief in immortality, was practically all that remained to him of the traditional Christian faith, and he affirmed it with a vigor that compensated for the abandonment of much else.

Theodore Parker is not in all respects typical of the liberal movement; but his discussion of Providence in *Theism, Atheism and the Popular Theology* is as clear and consistent a revelation of the logic of liberalism as

Calvin's discussion of it in the *Institutes* is a clear revelation of the logic of early Protestantism. As Calvin's faith was a militant faith, which gave assurance of the salvation of God's elect out of the hand of their enemies, so Parker's faith is a triumphant faith, which gives assurance that all is for the best in the best of all possible worlds. What he particularly abhors in the older theology is its doctrine of *Special Providence*, which seems to him to imply that God plays favorites, and takes better care of some of His children than of the rest. As against this, he asserts God's *Universal Providence*, which comprehends not only His government of the world, but His particular care for each individual part of the whole. Nothing, absolutely nothing, is finally to be lost. Every falling sparrow "falls to his bliss"; and every sinful act is a fall upward. As Calvin's doctrine follows logically from the conception of God as Absolute Will, together with a pessimistic judgment on the general course of events, so Parker's doctrine follows logically from the conception of God as Infinite Perfection and Infinite Power—together with an optimistic judgment on the course of events. A perfect and omnipotent God must needs make a perfect world, where pain and evil are present only in so far as they are necessary for educational purposes. And Parker, looking out upon his nineteenth-century world, has no difficulty in believing that it is perfect in the sight of God.

If we could overlook the cosmic forces which make up the material world [he writes] we should see that every actual storm and every rock was needful; and the world would not be perfect and accomplish its function had not each been put there in its proper time and place.

An oak-tree in the woods appears quite imperfect. The leaves are coiled up and spoiled by the leaf-roller . . . the twigs are sucked by the white-lined tree-hopper . . . the horn-hug, the curculio, and the timber-beetle eat up its wood . . . the grub lives in the young acorn . . . the creeper and the woodpecker bore through the bark . . . the bear dwells in its trunk which worms, emmets, bees, and countless insects have helped to hollow. . . . The carpenter cannot get a beam, the millwright a shaft, or the shipbuilder, a solid knee for his purpose; even the common woodman spares that tree as not worth felling; it only cumbers the ground. But it has served its complicated purpose. . . . It has been a great woodland caravansary, even a tavern and chateau, to all that heterogeneous swarm; and . . . no doubt the good God is quite contented with His oak, and says "Well done, good and faithful servant."

We commonly look on the world as the carpenter and millwright on that crooked oak, and because it does not serve our turn completely we think it an imperfect world. Thus men grumble at the rocky shores of New England . . . complain of wild beasts in the forests . . . and many a loathsome thing—hideous to our imperfect eye. How little do we know! a world without an alligator, or a rattlesnake, or a hyena, or a shark, would doubtless be a very imperfect world. The good God has something for each of these to do; a place for them all at His table, and a pillow for every one of them in Nature's bed.[2]

What lies behind Parker's optimism, and that of all the liberals of his generation, is a great new idea, an idea peculiar to modern times, the idea of Progress. The Renaissance did not believe in Progress, any more

[2] Parker, *Works*, Vol. XI, pp. 177, 178 (second edition), London, Trübner, 1867.

than the Reformation did; it looked back with reverence to classical antiquity, as the Reformation looked back to the Bible. But with the growth of the scientific spirit, the daring idea began to dawn upon men's minds that they were actually the superiors of the ancients by virtue of their steadily growing stock of knowledge; and they began to look ahead for the Golden Age instead of looking back. In Bacon's *New Atlantis*, the idea of Progress was already foreshadowed; in the "Quarrel between the Ancients and the Moderns," which broke out in France toward the end of the seventeenth century, the idea was definitely launched; in Condorcet's *History of the Progress of the Human Spirit*, written during the French Revolution, it found its classical expression.

The result of my work will be to show [says Condorcet] by reasoning and by facts, that there is no limit set to the perfecting of the powers of man; that human perfectibility is in reality indefinite; that the progress of this perfectibility, henceforth independent of any power that might wish to stop it, has no other limit than the duration of the globe upon which nature has placed us. Doubtless this progress can proceed at a pace more or less rapid, but it will never go backward.[3]

In its pure form, as stated by Condorcet, the idea of Progress was incompatible with the idea of Providence, for it implied man's power to achieve his own perfection and to master his own destiny by his own efforts, without divine aid. To Condorcet, religion and priestcraft were among the chief obstacles that blocked the

[3] Condorcet, *op. cit.*, Epoch I, quoted in Randall, *Making of the Modern Mind*, p. 383.

way to that continuous spread of enlightenment upon which the progress of the race depends. But there were other interpreters of the idea of Progress who gave to it a more religious turn. Lessing in his essay on *The Education of the Human Race* claimed that the whole history of mankind discloses a continuous advance in wisdom and virtue under divine leading and guidance. Divine revelation is to the race what education is to the individual; and the Old and New Testaments mark but two stages, already superseded, in God's never-ending revelation of new truth. Herder in his *Philosophy of History* said that "Genuine progress, constant development . . . is the purpose of God in history";[4] and his identification of Progress with Providence gave the cue to Schelling and Hegel, who likewise saw in the whole sweep of history the operation of "one increasing purpose," at once natural, human, and divine.

It was from these idealistic philosophers that American liberal theologians, from Parker and Bushnell to George A. Gordon, inherited their conception of Progressive Revelation and Progressive Providence. In later days, to be sure, the liberal faith in a kindly Providence received a severe shock from Darwinian evolution, with its portrait of "nature red in tooth and claw"; but it proved possible to justify the groaning and travailing of creation by appealing to the future glory of the sons of God, as Nietzsche on his part appealed to the coming Superman. John Fiske boldly turned the flank of scientific skepticism by adopting

[4] Quoted in McGiffert, *The Rise of Modern Religious Ideas*, pp. 173-174.

Herbert Spencer's evolutionary naturalism as the foundation-stone of an optimistic faith in God. Surely, he argued, if Spencer is right in his faith that evolution automatically makes for the growth of altruism and the growth of freedom, we have a right to interpret the evolutionary process as the ongoing thrust of the will of a beneficent Deity. After Darwinism, as before, the liberal conception of Providence is that of a great process of education, which brings all men at last to the light. Thus George A. Gordon in his *Ultimate Conceptions of Faith* writes as follows:

Between the physical organism of man and his environment there is an increasing harmony. Natural selection means nothing less. . . . The time may come when there shall be no more pain. . . . A better economic condition has come; a better still is bound to come. . . . God's world-plan is the education of mankind; that is the great assumption of religious faith. . . . And along with this vision of the educative purpose of God for the individual life there is the sense of the world-process for the recovery of sight to the blind. History is seen to be inexorably just, and for this reason infinitely kind. . . . The ancient blunder of self-seeking will not always be repeated; the joy of existence will not forever be sought for, against the whole protest of the past, in impossible fields. Light will, in the overwhelming majority of cases, be welcome, and darkness will be disowned. . . . Optimism is a faith that has good foundations.[5]

[5] George A. Gordon, *Ultimate Conceptions of Faith,* pp. 238-248. New York, Houghton Mifflin, 1903. Quoted by permission. As an example of the mingling of the ideas of Providence and Progress in pre-war American thought, I may be permitted to cite the peroration of a youthful speech against militarism which I delivered in a high-school debate in the year 1913. No amount of argument could save militarism from destruction, I said, for it stood in the way of "that mighty, irresistible onrolling force which some men call Progress

2. PROVIDENCE IN AN AGE OF REALISM

If the doctrine of Providence was equally dear to the pioneers of the Reformation, and the pioneers of liberal Protestantism, it must be confessed that its present status is much more problematical. The Age of Realism is not ringing with the strains of *Ein' Feste Burg*, nor accompanying the "march of Progress" with triumphant *Te Deums*. Between George A. Gordon and Reinhold Niebuhr, a change has come over the spirit of our times, and the old faiths and hopes no longer carry conviction, when stated in the old terms.

Certainly we have every motive for believing in divine Providence today, if we honestly can. *Human* providence, in which Condorcet put his trust when he so confidently proclaimed the inevitability and irreversibility of Progress, has somehow slipped a cog in these late years; and the great machine of industrial civilization, which seemed but a few years ago to be carrying us steadily up the incline toward some terrestrial paradise, is now rushing madly down the track again, careening from side to side and apparently headed for destruction, despite all that our engineers and brakemen can do to slacken its speed. No doubt our bewilderment and despair have lightened somewhat since they reached their nadir-point in the early months of 1933. Since March Fourth of that year the "ghost

---

and other men call Providence, but all men alike respect." I remember that peroration verbatim, because it was delivered with great fervor and appeared to strike fire with the audience at the time, whereas within a twelvemonth afterwards it began to ring ironically in my inward ear.

of indecision" has been laid, and we are at least doing
something about our plight. Destruction is apparently
not so imminent as we feared, and there is still time to
try various mechanical devices aiming to stop the de-
scent. But in our serious moments, as we weigh the
results of our leaders' policies, we still tend to agree
with the somber estimates of our situation to which
such cautious thinkers as Colonel House gave voice in
the early months of '33.

It is footless [wrote Colonel House] to say that this or
that cannot happen in times like these. The minds of our
people are in a ferment and things which we would have
declared impossible a few years ago are in actual process of
coming about. One of the causes of unrest is the almost
complete lack of confidence in our political and financial
leaders.

In other ages like this, when human leadership has
proved insufficient and humanity has found itself in
the grip of forces beyond its comprehension or control,
there has arisen a swelling tide of aspiration toward
God, trust in God's overruling Providence, eagerness
to know his Will and to do it. This time, it is not so.
There is every reason to expect a revival of religion in
times like these, but somehow it does not come. What
is the impediment? Why do men not commit themselves
once more to the care of Providence, as the Reformers
did, and so ride out this storm, too, with calm and
serene minds?

It would take a prophet rather than a theologian to
give the adequate answer to such questions. The causes
of belief and unbelief lie far below the intellectual

level, in the region of men's inchoate gropings and imaginings. Yet a partial answer may be given in intellectual terms. *Providence, in most men's minds, implies something reliable and protective in the natural and social orders, which is at the same time a source of guidance and strength to the individual.* A generation ago, the great problem was to discern the working of Providence in the *natural* order; today, thanks to liberal theology, the science-religion dualism is surmounted and the way is fairly clear to a spiritual interpretation of nature. But between the natural order and the inner life—where each man may and must discover the Providence of God for himself—there stands the apparently impenetrable barrier of the *social* order, which hides the face of the God of nature, and makes the God of grace, the God of the inner life, seem a feeble interloper in His own world.

There is very little in our present social order that naturally suggests the Providence of God: that, I believe, is the major reason for the present decline of faith in Providence. When man lived close to nature, and felt his human efforts supported by the cosmic powers of sun and rain, seed and soil, he found in all this an appropriate symbol of divine love and care, and spontaneously reacted with an attitude of grateful dependence. The modern city-dweller may ultimately be as dependent upon nature as his rural cousin, but he does not feel his dependence; and the goods which come to his apartment up the dumb-waiter are delivered by persons who care as little for him as he cares for them. In feudal society, a man's relation to his overlord was not always ideal, but it was at least personal and organic, so that loyalty and trust easily passed up the feudal ladder, through King and Emperor and Pope, to rest at last in a God whose Providence seemed to pervade the whole system. In modern industrial society, a man's relation to the great corporation that employs him is impersonal and mechanical. He seeks his own interests; the firm seeks its own interests; between them there is only what has been called a "cash nexus," which is as often a source of conflict as of unity. Our whole society is strong in mechanical efficiency, weak in controlling purpose and organic fellowship. It is hard to conceive that such a depersonalized social order has any divine animating spirit at all; if it has, then the God who rules it is a very snobbish and exclusive deity, partial to a few favorites and placidly indifferent to the suffering multitudes! How such a Deity would look, if definitely visualized, is perhaps indicated by some savagely satirical verses which Edmund Wilson recently wrote for the *New Yorker*, apropos of Struthers Burt's testimony that he still felt "the keen swift faith that God is good." Meditating on this remark, Mr. Wilson confesses that he felt a rising sense of resentment:

And felt the keen swift faith, I will assert,
That God was pretty good to Struthers Burt!
—For God and Struthers Burt are gentlefolks:
They differ from Jack Dempsey and Joe Doaks.
God is a big beneficent trustee,
Who asks well-bred professors in to tea;
Has swans and swimming-pools around his grounds;
Collects old books, and sometimes rides to hounds.

God was a club or two ahead of Burt,
But not enough to make him cold or curt. . . .
God sometimes has Burt stay with him for weeks,
And utters fierce shrill Philadelphian squeaks.[6]

What these verses may signify concerning Struthers
Burt and Edmund Wilson is beside the point. But they
do make it plain that to picture God as one of the well-
to-do rulers of our present social system is to commit
blasphemy, and pave the way for an atheistic revolt.
Now, consciously or unconsciously, our contemporaries
are committing just this blasphemy. They are assuming
that the Providence of God is, of course, on the side
of the existing social structure, and whatever weakens
the *status quo* impugns the divine authority. "God is
a big benevolent trustee," whose ruling passion is for
Order and Prosperity; so that His prestige will be irre-
parably impaired unless we very soon get back to "normalcy," as of the years 1920-1929!

There is much in the history of the idea of Providence that gives color to this absurd assumption. When
the Stoics talked about Providence, they meant to imply that the world was so perfectly designed by divine
reason that it would be impiety to seek to improve
upon it. "A wise and good man, after examining these
things," says Epictetus, "submits his mind to him who
administers the whole, as good citizens do to the laws
of the commonwealth."[7] When the Protestant Reformers talked about Providence, they spoke indeed as rebels
against the Catholic Church, but they made up in rev-

[6] *The New Yorker*, March 17, 1934, p. 21. Quoted by permission.
[7] Epictetus, *Discourses,* Chapter XII, "Of Contentment" (Every-
man Ed., p. 29).

erence for other constituted authorities what they lacked in reverence for the Church. Had not St. Paul said that "the powers that be are ordained of God"? Listening to Luther denouncing the Peasants' Revolt, or to Calvin rebuking rebels against the laws of the most Christian city of Geneva, one gets the strong impression that God and the police are somehow leagued together, and civil disobedience always constitutes reprehensible behavior in the eyes of the Almighty. More recently, our liberal doctrine of Providence has been suggesting that we live in a progressively improving world, where optimism is the only rational and pious attitude, and pessimism is evidence of a diseased mind. In the face of all these precedents, it is not surprising that popular faith in Providence is declining with the declining power and prestige of our present social system. "The Lord will provide" means something very definite to the average American; it means steady employment and a "full dinner-pail"; and unless the Lord can provide these things again very shortly, it looks as though our trust in Providence had been misplaced.

Now if there is anything at all in the ancient Hebrew faith in the coming Kingdom of God, wherein "the meek inherit the earth," this whole way of looking at Providence is a ghastly mistake. Before God's Will can be done on earth, there must be a drastic change in our human institutions; and the Providence of God may at certain times be far better seen in the forces that demolish a corrupt social order, and sweep away its débris, than in those that attempt to preserve its crumbling institutions. To adopt a striking simile of Karl

Marx, there come times when the new order is struggling to free itself from the old like a butterfly struggling to burst out of its chrysalis. Shall the Providence of God, in such a time, be identified with the forces that seek to keep the old skin from splitting, or the new life that insists on splitting the skin? Shall God be cast perpetually in the rôle of a reactionary, and never in the rôle of a revolutionary?

If we can detach our minds momentarily from our own social situation, the whole matter may perhaps appear to us in a more just perspective. A friendly critic, who prefers to remain anonymous, has lately made some interesting observations on Christianity in the Far East. He remarks that Christianity in China has been most commonly presented as "the way out" for China; and since for most Chinese "the way out" implies "the recovery of the four Eastern provinces and driving the Japanese off the Asiatic mainland," the failure of the League and the "Christian" nations to accomplish these objectives seems like a failure of divine Providence and a crushing disproof of the power of the Christian religion.

Astonishing as it may seem [says this observer] even the most intelligent of these men never seem to have been haunted by the question: "Is it possible that God's way out for China may be something different from the way out which we desire?" . . . The idea of the Suffering Servant and even more of the Suffering Nation purified by its captivity is not a part of Chinese Christian thought. The suggestion that God's Will for China might be through the valley of defeat and humiliation is a scandal for the acceptance of which the teaching of their intellectual leaders has not prepared the Christian Community, and which seems utterly contrary to what they had been led to believe Christianity would do for them.

Now it ill becomes American Christians to throw stones at Chinese Christians, or to offer them advice in a patronizing manner. The evils of economic imperialism from which they are suffering, and the superficial optimism which unfits them to face these evils, are both Western importations into the Orient. But it is easier to see in their case than in our own that "God's way out" may, indeed, be a path very different from the path of our dreams. It may be that no nation is really "grown up" until it has been purged of egotism and pride through humiliation and defeat, until it has trodden the rocky path that was worn by the feet and stained with the blood of God's first "chosen people," the Jews. It is not only China that must tread that path; Japan must tread it, and America must tread it too.

Perhaps we shall escape, this time. Perhaps America will survive not only this "First World War" and this first general depression but other world wars and other depressions as well, without any fundamental change in her manner of living or in her ideals. Perhaps we shall go on, like the children of Israel in the days of their independence, making good resolutions in every time of adversity and breaking them in every time of prosperity. We should not rejoice too much at such delays and postponements. We have a baptism to be baptized withal, and how are we straitened until it is accomplished! Until the bumptious, overconfident spirit of our youthful nation is humbled and tempered in some fiery furnace of suffering, we shall not be fit to enter into the universal Society of Nations—and we shall not understand the true doctrine of Providence. For the true doctrine of Providence is not that of the liberal Protestants, nor that of the Reformers, nor that of the Stoics, but that of the Prophets and the Apostles. I suggest that we look at that ancient doctrine closely, and see if it be as incredible and as unrealistic as our age is apt to suppose.

3. THE PROPHETIC AND APOSTOLIC DOCTRINE OF PROVIDENCE

The Hebrew prophets are sometimes regarded as romantic dreamers, dwelling in another world as an escape from the grim realities of this one. Speaking of the idea of the "Day of Yahweh" or "coming of the Kingdom" which runs like a *leit-motif* through the history of Hebrew prophecy, Professor W. K. Wright says flatly, "The whole idea has always been visionary and fantastic."[8] The age of apocalypticism no doubt gave birth to many feverish and other-worldly dreams, some of them romantically impossible of fulfillment, some of them grotesquely bitter and vengeful. But the great writing prophets of the pre-exilic and exilic periods cannot thus lightly be dismissed. They were visionaries, indeed, who judged contemporary politics in terms of moral and religious principles, and discerned the Providence of God in everything; but their writings have been preserved to us mainly because their successors were convinced that they were the only clear-

[8] Wright, *Student's Philosophy of Religion*, p. 145.

seeing and right-seeing men of their time, whose insight and foresight had been abundantly justified by subsequent events. In an age of social disintegration very like our own, they alone correctly read the signs of the times.

This quality of clear vision is especially evident in the case of the first of the prophetic line, upon whose basic concept of God's incorruptible and impartial justice all the later prophets built their further affirmations. Amos, the herdsman of Tekoa, was a realist in every sense of the word. He differed from his contemporaries mainly in his ability to discern the ominous signs of impending disaster to which they were comfortably and sleepily indifferent, and to link these ominous signs with that same righteous judgment of God which they were eager and willing to see visited upon their enemies or their neighbors. Sham piety and swollen prosperity could not deceive his sharp eyes; he perceived that the piety was insincere and immoral, the prosperity based upon injustice and extortion.

It is of the utmost significance [says George Adam Smith] that this reformer, this founder of the highest order of prophecy in Israel, should not only thus begin with facts, but to the very end be occupied with almost nothing else, than the vision and record of them. . . . The new prophecy which Amos started in Israel reached Divine heights of hope. . . . But it started from the truth about the moral situation of the present. Its first prophet not only denied every popular dogma and ideal, but appears not to have substituted for them any others. He spent his gifts of vision on the discovery and appreciation of facts. . . . We are constantly disposed to abuse even the most just and necessary of religious ideals as substitutes for experience or as escapes from duty, and to boast about the future before we have understood or mastered the present. Hence the need of realists like Amos.[9]

I believe that George Adam Smith is right in his claim that the prophetic vision of Amos was a vision of the truth; and I should add that the truth which he saw is a truth not only about the Kingdom of Israel, but about any social order whatsoever. What that truth was, is best suggested by the vision which stands dramatically apart from all the other visions in the Book of Amos, because it led directly to the prophet's being rebuked and denounced to the King by Amaziah, priest of Bethel:

> The Lord Eternal showed me this,
> showed me himself standing beside a wall,
> a plumb-line in his hand.
> The Eternal said to me,
> "Amos, what do you see?"
> "A plumb-line," I replied.
> The Eternal said, "With a plumb-line I test my people;
> never again will I pardon them,
> but Isaac's heights shall be laid waste,
> the shrines of Israel shall be ruined,
> and I will attack Jeroboam's house with the sword."[10]

The plumb-line which the prophet saw so many centuries ago was no figment of the imagination. It was really there. It has never ceased to be there. For our

[9] George Adam Smith, *The Book of the Twelve Prophets* (Expositor's Bible), Vol. I, pp. 85, 86 (fifth edition). New York, Armstrong and Son, 1899. Quoted by permission of Harper & Brothers, present publishers.

[10] Amos 7:7-9. From *The Holy Bible,* a new translation by James Moffatt. New York, Harper & Brothers.

modern nationalistic Amaziahs, as for all their proto-
types, it is doubtless heretical and treasonable to suggest that any final disaster could possibly overtake our
country or our type of civilization; but whoever has
moral insight may still see the God of the plumb-line
standing in our midst, testing our institutions by the
canons of social justice, and condemning to destruction whatever is not "on the square." Even to the
morally blind, the sound of His work of demolition
must have been plainly audible in these last years and
months: crashing banks and crashing reputations, crashing political overturns, snapping and cracking of sup-
posedly stout timbers high and low throughout the
structure of our social order, and rumbling thunder of
approaching wars in the distance, before whose whirl-
wind no flimsy, sagging edifice can hope to stand.

It is a stern doctrine, this prophetic doctrine of the
plumb-line; but in times like ours it permits one to
face the future with a certain calmness. Things may be
going to pieces; but they are not going chaotically or
meaninglessly to pieces. There is method in this mad-
ness, justice in this destruction. Roughly and inexactly,
because of the crudity of the instruments of destruction
which must be used, God is at work "making the wrath
of men to praise him." There is no heat nor anger about
his Providence, nothing but a steady resistance of the
moral structure of things to all attempts to pull it out
of plumb. God stands erect, unswerving, holding the
line; what falls falls by its own weight and deserves
to fall, though it may carry much that is good and

beautiful down with it in its collapse. Our universe is "on the square."

At the close of the second year of the depression, John Haynes Holmes preached a sermon entitled "The Good in Bad Times," which to many of us was both clarifying and heartening. The best thing about such a time as this, he urged, was that it demonstrated clearly *"that we still live in a moral universe in which moral laws are not without avail."*[11] Supposing that it had been possible for the Great War, with its orgy of hatred and violence, to "come and go, and everything still proceed exactly as before," would it not have meant that we lived in a senseless and immoral world? Supposing that it had been possible for an economic order based upon self-interest and greed to perpetuate itself without ever leading to disaster, would it not have meant that the God of the prophets was a pure illusion?

And now [says Dr. Holmes] when I see the whole structure of our Western life suddenly collapsing and falling into ruin, when I see the machinery which we have builded failing to perform even the basic function of keeping people alive, am I wrong in seeing the triumph of that spiritual idealism which has long since condemned our capitalistic order as the "abomination of desolation"? The triumph is bought, if you will, at a terrific price. It is the price of the comfort, happiness, health, prosperity, even lives, of millions of men and women. The dissolution of our society, now steadily going forward, may sooner or later involve us all in unimaginable disaster. But is even such a price too heavy to pay for the vindication of the truth that there is a road that leadeth, broad and smooth, unto destruction, and a road that leadeth,

[11] John Haynes Holmes, *The Sensible Man's View of Religion,* p. 100. New York, Harper & Brothers. Quoted by permission.

straight and narrow, unto life? What we see in these menaces of our time is the unshaken integrity of our moral order. The stars in their courses are still preserved from wrong.[12]

I do not mean to assert, and I am sure Dr. Holmes does not mean to assert, that the Hebrew prophets were infallible in all their insights, or that even their deepest insights went to the bottom of things. Amos seriously confused the moral with the natural order when he saw the divine retribution working through earthquakes and plagues of locusts. Some of the earlier prophets, still under the sway of nationalistic prejudice, lent their authority to the belief that Jerusalem was inviolable and could never be taken by a foreign enemy. Had events continued to support this theory, as they supported a similar theory among the Japanese at the time of the Mongol invasions, the religion of Israel might never have developed into a genuine monotheism, but remained pent up, like some types of Shintoism, in a narrow nationalistic pride.[13] A still more serious error, already mentioned in the preceding chapter, was the tendency among many of the prophets to assert that the sufferings of individuals and nations are exactly proportionate to their guilt. This ignores, of course, the great law of social solidarity, which makes the innocent to suffer with the guilty, and indeed to suffer *more* than the guilty, in proportion to their moral and religious sensitiveness. But experience, and the insight

[12] *Ibid.*, pp. 103, 104.
[13] See Kato's *Study of Shinto, the Religion of the Japanese Nation,* Chapter XIX, "Some Deeper Reflections upon the Divine Protection of the Nation," where the course of events in Israel is compared with the course of events in Japan.

of other prophets, corrected most of these errors. Jeremiah—and Nebuchadnezzar!—settled the question of the inviolability of Jerusalem; and Isaiah 53, together with the Book of Job, made it inexcusable thenceforth to draw an exact equivalence between sin and suffering. Taking the prophetic teaching about the Providence of God as a whole, I think it must be said that its truth still holds; and the evidence thereof is the fact that it still enables those who are guided by its principles to read the signs of the times more correctly and see more deeply into the mystery of the future than most of their contemporaries. Consider, as a fine example, these extraordinary words of George Adam Smith, inspired by his study of Amos, and uttered many years before the World War, when most of his contemporaries were still confident of the inevitability of Progress:

That there exist among us means of new historic convulsions is a thing hard for us to admit. But the signs cannot be hid. When we see the jealousies of the Christian peoples, and their enormous preparations for battle; the arsenals of Europe which a few sparks may blow up; the millions of soldiers one man's word may mobilise; when we imagine the opportunities which a general war would furnish to the discontented masses of the European proletariat,—we must surely acknowledge the existence of forces capable of inflicting calamities, so severe as to affect not merely this nationality or that type of culture, but the very vigour and progress of civilization herself; and all this without our looking beyond Christendom, or taking into account the rise of the yellow races to a consciousness of their approach to equality with ourselves. If, then, in the eyes of the Divine justice Christendom merits judgment,—if life continue to be left so hard to the poor, . . . if we continue to pour the evils of our civilization upon the barbarian, and "the vices of our young nobles," to paraphrase Juvenal, "are aped in" Hindustan,—then let us know that the means of a judgment more awful than any which has yet scourged a delinquent civilisation are extant and actual among us.[14]

These words were first spoken from a Scottish pulpit, before appearing in print in 1896. One can imagine the kind of reception they got: the admiring comments on the dominie's vivid rhetoric; the wagging of heads and tongues over the question whether it might actually be possible for this civilization to fare like all the others; the utter inability to believe that anything serious could happen to the world, while the British Empire was there to police it. And yet that scholar-preacher was speaking the exact, unvarnished truth about what was to transpire during his own lifetime: God's truth, mediated to him through the prophet Amos.

That is to say, *one side of God's truth.* There is, of course, another side to the Biblical doctrine of Providence, less grim and more hopeful. It is only implicit in the teaching of Amos, whose last authentic words are words of unrelieved doom and disaster. It is only suggested here and there in the pre-exilic prophets, who were for the most part occupied in arousing a lethargic people to a proper sense of their danger. But when the disaster of the Exile has fallen at last, and the first shock of it has been borne, there begins a new chorus of hopeful prophecy, which rises higher and

[14] George Adam Smith, *The Book of the Twelve Prophets,* Vol. I, p. 154. Quoted by permission.

higher in its confidence, until at length in the New
Testament it becomes a pæan of thanksgiving for hopes
fulfilled and victory assured. The Day of the Lord,
which to Amos was a Day of Doom, has become a
Day of Deliverance, and everlasting life and joy are
promised to all who will confess the name of the
Deliverer.

As the prophetic doctrine of Providence is typically
expressed in the teaching of Amos, so the apostolic
doctrine of Providence is typically expressed in the
teaching of St. Paul. As Amos lived in a period of social
disintegration strangely like our own, so did St. Paul.
In Amos's time, the Northern Kingdom of Israel was
ripe for destruction; in Paul's time, the terrible days
of the siege and destruction of Jerusalem, and the final
dispersion of the Jewish people, were just ahead.

Can it be said of St. Paul, as of Amos, that he was
a sound, realistic observer of the signs of his times;
or must it be confessed that he was in some respects
"visionary and fantastic"? Certainly it cannot be claimed
that he possessed the kind of insight into the trend of
public affairs which Amos and Isaiah possessed. With
the loss of political independence, that kind of insight
had long since waned and disappeared in Israel; indeed, it could hardly be said to exist anywhere in the
vast horde of alien peoples whom Rome had subjected
to her rule. Whenever Paul, or any of his contemporaries, speaks of coming political events, he speaks in
a language of vague mystic symbolism, which shows
that he is not at home in that field. Nowhere does he
suggest that he has any such ability to forecast the

political future as Amos exhibited when he predicted that the Ten Tribes of Israel would be carried into captivity by the Assyrians. Instead of a revolt, a siege, a massacre, and a dispersion, he expects to see the temporary triumph of Antichrist, who will lead many astray with spurious miracles and fair words, until suddenly, just when matters are at their worst,

The Lord himself will descend from heaven with a loud summons, when the archangel calls and the trumpet of God sounds; the dead in Christ will rise first; then we the living, who survive, will be caught up along with them in the clouds to meet the Lord in the air, and so we shall be with the Lord forever.[15]

No, Paul's insight did not lie in the field of politics. In this field, he not only erred, but erred wildly and extravagantly, like most of his contemporaries; and it is unfortunate in many ways that the record of his apocalyptic fancies has remained in writing, to tempt the uneducated to similar unfounded hopes, in every season of hard times. The best that can be said of these hopes is that they do reflect the ancient assurance that the universe is squarely built, so that when matters get too bad some great revolution is bound to occur, from which the "humble and meek" may expect to profit. But if Paul's political insight was weak, that does not mean that he was devoid of clear vision. In the realm

[15] I Thess. 4:16, 17, from *The Holy Bible*, a new translation by James Moffatt. New York, Harper & Brothers. It is true that the apocalyptic element in St. Paul's teaching, which bulks so large in the Thessalonian letters, diminishes steadily in the later letters; but this does not argue any improvement in his political insight. It only testifies to his increasing preoccupation with the inward life of the Christian fellowship.

of the inner life, the realm of the Spirit, he was a master and a genius; and in that realm he discovered truths that were hidden from the more external vision of the early prophets. Among these truths none was more important than that which he expressed in that famous verse from the Eighth of Romans, in which his whole doctrine of Providence is summed up: "And we know that all things work together for good to them that love God, to them who are the called according to his purpose."[16]

The doctrine of Providence here implied differs from the prophetic doctrine of Providence in that it has to do with what is called *special Providence*: a special guidance and protection which God extends only to those who are possessed of His Spirit, and living in accordance with His Will. Such special Providence implies and includes a *particular Providence* (extending to the most detailed concerns of individual life) of which Amos knew nothing, but of which Jeremiah and Ezekiel had intimations, and of which Jesus was serenely confident, when he said that the very hairs of our head are all numbered. It was St. Paul's conviction, based evidently upon direct experience and observation, that when a man came into relation with that strange divine energy of life which the New Testament calls "the Spirit," he found himself lifted above the level of general Providence, upon which even the greatest of the early prophets dwelt, and transported into a "realm of grace" where his poor powers were mar-

[16] Rom. 8:28. Moffatt translates somewhat freely as follows: "We know also that those who love God, those who have been called in terms of his purpose, have his aid and interest in everything."

velously reinforced, his halting reason was infused with heavenly wisdom, and his sense of failure and guilt was replaced with a humble sense of acceptance and forgiveness. To such an one, the political future might be veiled in mystery and the fortunes of every day full of perils and vicissitudes, but nothing could disturb his calm, since nothing could separate him from the love of God.

The doctrine of special Providence has been sharply attacked by many liberals, as both immoral and superstitious. Theodore Parker regarded it as the last vestige of the outworn notion of miracle, and railed against the notion that a perfectly benevolent God could prefer one of His creatures over any other. As a corrective to the favoritism and provincialism which narrow and pervert the Reformation doctrine of Providence, and which are present to some extent even in the New Testament, Parker's doctrine of universal Providence is most salutary. But he himself admits that God's universal Providence works otherwise in the animal world than in the material world and otherwise in man than in the animals.[17] Why then should it not work otherwise in the saint than in the sinner, otherwise in Jesus than in Judas? And why, above all, should we attempt to prescribe exactly how God's Providence *ought* to work, in terms of human analogies and *a priori* reasonings, instead of observing objectively just how it *does* work? Here is the prime difference between Parker's liberal theology and the realistic theology we seek to formulate: the one proceeds from *what ought to be* to

[17] *Op cit.,* p. 189.

what is; the other observes *what is* as broadly and deeply as possible, derives its ideals from deep-lying actualities, and returns constantly to actualities for the testing of its ideals.

A more serious objection to the doctrine of special Providence, from the realistic point of view, was offered by Mr. H. G. Wells in his remarkable war-time book, *God the Invisible King.* The ordinary Christian doctrine of Providence reminds him, he says, of Daudet's comic story, *Tartarin in the Alps,* in which the chicken-hearted hero is inspired to perform daring feats of mountaineering by being informed that all the precipices and crevasses in Switzerland are equipped with invisible nets, and he cannot possibly come to harm. There is much advantage in this theory, says Mr. Wells; it enables many timorous souls to get through life without quailing; but it has one serious disadvantage; it has no objective truth in it whatsoever. With Sir Francis Younghusband, he denies the reality of any "outside Providence, who created us, who watches over us, and who guides our lives like a Merciful Father"; instead of which, he joins with Sir Francis in affirming the reality of "a Holy Spirit, radiating upward through all animate beings," and inwardly accessible to man in his highest moments.

If you would fly into the air [says Mr. Wells] there is no God to bank your aeroplane correctly for you or keep an ill-tended engine going; if you would cross a glacier, no God nor angel guides your steps amidst the slippery places. . . . Nothing of such things will God do; it is an idle dream. But God will be with you nevertheless. In the reeling aeroplane or the dark ice-cave God will be your courage. Though you

suffer or are killed, it is not an end. He will be with you as
you face death; he will die with you as he has died already
countless myriads of brave deaths. He will come so close to
you that at the last you will not know whether it is you or
he who dies, and the present death will be swallowed up in
his victory.[18]

The only adequate Christian rejoinder to these words
of Mr. Wells is, "Amen!" If there are any individuals
who hold the Tartarin-in-the-Alps theory of Providence
—and doubtless there are some—they are not apostolic
Christians. St. Paul himself is so close to the position
of Mr. Wells that the words last quoted might easily
be taken as a commentary on the Eighth of Romans.
Paul clearly does not expect to be guarded from all
evil by a God who "spared not his own Son." Anguish,
calamity, persecution, famine, nakedness, danger, and
death are all to be expected, in the course of the Christian life. But in the midst of these trials, we may be
sustained by the inward presence of a Spirit that "as-
sists us in our weakness," "pleads for us with groan-
ings that cannot be uttered," and unites us in indissolu-
ble bonds of love with a Life that is more enduring and
worthful than our own little lives can be by themselves,
alone.

Basically, then, Paul and Mr. Wells are in agreement
in what they affirm about God's relation to man. It is
primarily an inward relation of Spirit with spirit, which
offers no guaranty of external success or prosperity.
But Mr. Wells goes on to deny that God is in any sense

[18] *God the Invisible King*, pp. 38, 39. (See the whole section, pp.
35-39, entitled "God Is Not Providence.") New York, Macmillan,
1917. Quoted by permission.

at work in the external world, while Paul believes, as truly as Amos, that God is at work there, too, and believes that there is a marvelous interaction between God's inner and outer activity, between His special and general Providence. If the life of the Christian is not immune from danger and distress, it is nevertheless led and fortified in many extraordinary ways. Paul must have been convinced that his own life, full of hairbreadth escapes, was inexplicable except upon the theory that God guides and protects His chosen emissaries until they have accomplished their mission.

Now, at the risk of appearing guilty of romanticism and superstition, I wish to say that at this point I believe Paul is right and Mr. Wells is wrong. There *is* such a thing as special guidance and protection for those who are willing to be God's instruments, and do His Will. Things *do* "work together for good" for them, in extraordinary ways. While not exempted from illness and death, they seem to have charmed lives. They move unharmed among brigands and drunkards; they minister to the diseased without catching the infection; they survive beatings and illnesses of which others die; and the sting of death, when it comes, is removed for them. I do not speak rhetorically nor imaginatively; I have known such people myself. Their extraordinary immunity can be explained in part, no doubt, by the effect of their courageous and radiant personalities upon their own physical powers of resistance and upon the attitudes of the people with whom they meet; but I am convinced there is more to it than that. While I recognize the dangers of the doctrine of "guidance," if it leads to the disparagement of reason and common sense, I believe that there is realistic ground for the conviction that prevails in the Salvation Army and the Oxford Group Movement, that more than human power and wisdom are available for him who rightly adjusts himself to the Will of God, and what he does under such control fits in with the other plans of God, to form a connected series of events that is more than coincidence. Especially among the Quakers, I believe I have felt and tested for myself what this higher power and wisdom are like. To anyone who regards this as pure moonshine I would simply say, Get any good account of the work and faith of the Salvation Army, such as Hugh Redwood's *God in the Slums*, consider the multiple instances of special "calls" and "leadings" there related, and meditate on the significance of words like these, in which Mr. Redwood sketches the faith of the typical Salvation Army lassie:

Talk with a slum-officer for five minutes and you will find that she speaks of God as one having direct knowledge of Him and direct access to His presence. She is satisfied that she lives under His very real protection, for which reason she is not afraid, in case of need, to penetrate, alone and by night, into streets which policemen traverse only in twos and threes. . . . She believes, indeed she *knows* from repeated experience, that in times of emergency she will be endowed with superhuman faculties of endurance . . .

She is no fanatic: the God in whom she puts this absolute trust, to Whom and of Whom she speaks with a frankness and a familiarity oftentimes a little discomposing to those unused to it, is a God Who expects His children to be tolerant and patient, to be mindful of the ordinary rules of hygiene—not forgetting that a healthy appetite is something to be grateful for—to share and to develop the gift of laughter, and at all times to employ the common sense with which He has equipped them.[19]

A person like this is a living proof of the apostolic doctrine of Providence.

4. THE TWO HANDS OF GOD'S PROVIDENCE: LAW AND GRACE

It may be affirmed, then, as a reasonable faith that in two distinct ways the Providence of God is a reality to be reckoned with: as a general impersonal principle of justice, like that perceived by the prophets; and as a dynamic principle of saving grace, like that experienced by the apostles. Two great superhuman processes seem to run through history: a grim process of action and reaction, in which the proud and cruel are usually victorious, and then meet Nemesis by overreaching themselves; and a quiet mysterious process of assimilation wherein the men of God win their way, against appalling obstacles, by soul-force alone. Neither of these processes guarantees the inevitability of Progress, since the former is purely negative and defensive, so to speak, and the latter is perpetually defeated by those who despise and reject the importunities of the Spirit; yet this much can be said with assurance, that we live in a world where the triumph of evil can never be complete, since evil systems eventually destroy themselves by their own greed and egotism, and the Spirit is never more persuasive than when it suffers silently,

[19] Hugh Redwood, *God in the Slums,* pp. 43, 44. New York, Fleming H. Revell Co., 1931. Quoted by permission.

unflinchingly, beneath the heel of oppression. Against the stone-wall defensive structure of God's elemental justice, earth's conquerors and exploiters hurl themselves eventually to their own destruction; against the power of God's forgiving love and grace, the hearts of evil men are never so fast-locked but that they may be captured by some sudden surprise attack.

That these two processes are part of one vast strategy of Providence is certainly not evident upon the face of things. One fully understands why Marcion failed to recognize the Old Testament God of justice as one and the same with the New Testament God of grace, and refused to worship the former. Is it tenable, one may ask, that God should be at once a God of wrath and a God of love? Has He two hands, one iron-gloved, the other warm and human? Is it conceivable that He should alternately woo us with the one and strike us with the other? Could we believe this, we might perhaps hear Him saying to our generation, in tones of mingled sorrow and anger, "You must and shall have deeper fellowship in your social order. You may take it *this* way (stretching out the right hand) or you may take it *this* way (clenching the left fist). If you will hear my Word, you may yet make the great soulless machine of your industrial civilization an instrument for the common good and a bond of fellowship between you; but if not, then I will smash your civilization, and reduce you to a more primitive level of existence where you *must* recover the art of fellowship, which your pioneering forefathers knew, and you have lost." Such a faith has great power of appeal to me, and I am persuaded that it is well grounded; yet it is full of bristling difficulties, which for me are resolved only because I see the gulf between the God of the clenched fist and the God of the outstretched hand bridged over by Christ and his Church.

We shall be occupied more than once, in the concluding chapters of this book, with the endeavor to resolve some features of this great paradox; but meanwhile let us simply recall, like good realists, the "irreducible and stubborn facts" which lie behind it and which must be accepted whether we can explain them or not. It is a fact that, as John Bennett puts it, "There are definite limits to human evil. When it has gone far enough it comes up against obstacles which make it necessary for men to change their ways."[20] And it is a fact that certain men who have given themselves whole-heartedly to the relief of human suffering and the upbuilding of human fellowship, have experienced an inward security which no misfortune can shake, and found external circumstances strangely "working together for good" on their behalf.

Neither of these facts is a *scientific* fact; let us be clear about that. Scientifically, the most that can be affirmed about the Providence of God is that the structure of reality exhibits a certain mathematical regularity and dependable sequence, which proves that our world is a cosmos and not a chaos. If the biological and social sciences be added to the physical, the conception of Providence is enriched by the notion of a vast ongoing tendency toward the creation of richer

[20] *The Christian Century*, November 8, 1933, p. 1405.

and richer organic wholes, moving upstream, so to speak, against the general physical tendency toward the degradation of energy.[21] There is no scientific assurance of a principle of moral justice in the world, precisely because science as such is indifferent to moral distinctions, as it is indifferent to all matters of value. But if science disregards moral distinctions, men and nations disregard them at their peril. To deny this fact is to be most unrealistic. None of the great political movements of our day is so timidly respectful to science that it dares not rest its weight upon convictions that have less than scientific certitude. If political movements were so meticulous as that, they would all perish of inanition. Surely it is time to announce to the clergy that the age of science—that is, the age when scientific precision was the one accepted criterion of truth—is over at last, and the age of social action is upon us. The work of scientific criticism must continue to be a part of the work of theology; but unless theology can issue in full-blooded convictions at least as capable of inspiring religious fervor and social passion as the convictions of the Nazis or the Communists, the theologians may as well shut up shop, and admit defeat. The conviction of the reality of the Providence of God is, I believe, a conviction that is fully capable of meeting that acid test.

[21] See Montague, *Belief Unbound,* pp. 70-74, and Van Dusen, *The Plain Man Seeks for God,* Chap. III.

CHAPTER IV

A REALISTIC ESTIMATE OF CHRIST AND THE CHURCH

EVERY religious system starts, as we saw in our second chapter, with some sort of diagnosis of our human predicament; and it ends, of course, with some concrete recommendations as to how to find the way out of our difficulties, toward some goal of attainment. It begins with an order to *halt*, in the presence of a threatening hostile force, and it ends with an order to *march*, in some clearly defined direction. But if the final marching orders are to be wise and effective, a good deal of reconnoitering must first be done. The strength of the hostile force must be estimated, the configuration of the surrounding country must be accurately mapped out, and all available reinforcements must be summoned.

We have still one more chapter of reconnoitering ahead of us, before announcing our "Plan of Salvation" in the concluding chapter. We have endeavored to reckon realistically with the dangers and difficulties of our human predicament. We have charted the cosmic terrain, and concluded that, thanks to the Providence of God, the general "lay of the land" and the powers of wind and wave are on our side, *if* we rightly shape our course to meet their inexorable requirements. And now, before ordering the advance, we have only to estimate the strength of all available reinforcements, and join forces with them. For us, as Christians, this means primarily to estimate the strength of Christ and the Church.

1. PROTESTANT INDIVIDUALISM AND THE NEW LOYALISM[1]

It must be admitted at once that Protestantism has laid comparatively little stress upon Christ and the Church. When Adolf Harnack, echoing a famous passage of St. Augustine, said that the whole Christian Gospel was a question of "God and the soul, the soul and its God"; when he went on to say that it could all be expressed in terms of a few simple ideas, "God the Father, Providence, the position of men as God's children, the infinite value of the human soul"; when he defined the Christian religion in an unforgettable phrase as "Eternal life in the midst of time, by the strength and under the eyes of God"[2]—he spoke both as a typical liberal, and as a typical Protestant. For it was characteristic of Protestantism from the very start, and still more characteristic of it in its liberal forms, that it tended to brush aside all intermediaries—priests and prelates; sacred images and sacred relics; saints, angels, archangels, and even the Blessed Virgin herself—and so set God and the individual immediately in one another's presence.

[1] The first draft of this section was worked out in an article called "Loyalties," contributed to the *Intercollegian* in the winter of 1933-34. Portions of that article are incorporated, with the consent of the editors, in the present version.

[2] Harnack, *What Is Christianity?* pp. 61, 74, 8. The passage from St. Augustine to which he alludes is found in the *Soliloquies*, Bk. I, chap. II (7).

Certainly it was not the intention of the Reformers
to disparage either Christ or the Church. As the early
Buddhists, in making a profession of their faith, announced that they "took their refuge" in the Buddha
and the Order, as well as in the Law, so the Protestant
Reformers continued to rest their faith in part upon
the atoning work of Christ and upon the ministrations
of the Church, as well as upon the eternal decrees of
Providence revealed in the Bible; but their great reliance was in Providence, as the great reliance of the early
Buddhists was in the Law, and in both cases the other
two divine resources tended to fall into second rank.
If divine Providence has singled me out as one of the
elect, I may be saved directly, according to Calvin, by
inward "illumination of the Spirit, without the intervention of any preaching," and, it would seem, without
pleading the merits of Christ, whose work has no saving
power except what is imparted to it by the decree and
ordinance of God.[3] Calvin was a very high Churchman
and laid great stress on the Atonement; but in such
teachings as these he made both Christ and the Church
implicitly unnecessary.

The work of abolishing intermediaries, begun by
the Reformers, was completed by the liberals—especially by the Unitarians. To Channing it seemed "un-
favorable to piety" to associate Christ with God, or to
maintain that God is brought into more forgiving relations with man through the work of Christ. To Emerson and Parker it seemed self-evident that the "accent
of the Holy Ghost" was audible to the inner ear of

[3] Calvin, *Institutes,* iv. 16. 19.

every rightly attuned soul; and Jesus was the prophet of the universal Godhood of Man.—"Was he not our brother; the son of man, as we are; the Son of God, like ourselves?"[4]—The last intermediary between the soul and God thus vanishes, and the modern individual stands erect and solitary upon his mountaintop of vision, gazing unabashed, unblinking, at the Sun of Righteousness, and conscious of no attendant cloud of witnesses.

Outside of Unitarianism, the liberal movement has, of course, been more cautious in what it has said about Christ; verbally, and often in all sincerity of spirit, it has vied with orthodoxy in heaping honors upon his sacred name; yet baldly stated, its affirmations about Christ may be reduced to this: that he revealed "supremely" and perhaps "uniquely" what God is forever and everywhere revealing through a million other channels; just as a service in church "supremely and uniquely" expresses the presence of God which is just as truly conveyed by a sunset or a poem. The banquet of God's grace, from this point of view, is spread with equal abundance in all times and places; the individual has only to sit down where he pleases and help himself.

More and more, as this attitude has become common, the conviction has grown that religion is a "private affair," concerning only the individual and his Maker. The Reformation had granted to the individual the "right of private judgment" upon the meaning of the authoritative Scriptures; the Enlightenment went further, and made the individual reason and conscience the final court of appeal, supreme over all external authorities.

[4] Parker, *Works,* Vol. VIII, p. 20.

In the modern liberal churches,[5] religious credos are no longer fighting slogans, rallying points for common loyalty and collective action; they are matters of private opinion, about which it is impolite to question a man. The liberal churches themselves have no corporate life, no common consciousness; they are collections of religious individuals, each carrying on his private and peculiar type of commerce with God, but occasionally gathering for worship in the same place, where they may listen to some exceptionally gifted preacher air his private religious opinions—after which they go their separate ways as before. All this reminds one much more of a stolid group of Stoics or an esoteric band of Neo-Platonists listening to an eminent pagan philosopher, than it reminds one of a group of early Christians assembled for a love-feast. To be a Christian, in those days, you *had* to leave the world and become a member of a new society; you could not simply enroll as a regular hearer of sermons, and practice your religion privately.

And this leads to another observation. Modern liberal Protestantism cannot be said, by any stretch of the imagination, to have "left the world." It points with pride to the fact that it has outgrown the mystic other-

---

[5] The characterization of the "liberal churches" which follows will probably be more resented than any other passage in this book. I am fully aware of the fact that there are many liberal churches which do not, even remotely, answer to this description. I am not attacking any specific persons or denominations; I am simply describing and denouncing, in the plainest language at my command, a *tendency* which is deep-rooted in the liberal movement, which can be acutely sensed in many liberal churches, and to which, whether I find it in myself or in others, I propose to give no quarter.

worldliness and ascetic *contemptus mundi* of the medieval Church. It smiles at the Puritans for their fear of worldly amusements, worldly adornments, and worldly conversation. It does not say so, but the truth of the matter is, it has become a worldly institution, a factor in contemporary culture. And that being the case, it is not surprising that its own strong individualism, inherited from the Reformation and the Enlightenment, has been reinforced and interfused with other forms of modern individualism: the "rugged individualism" of the pioneers, the laissez-faire individualism of modern political liberals, the self-indulgent individualism of the post-war age of self-expression, and many other brands as well. Small wonder that a distinguished missionary to the Orient remarked, after a visit to the United States, that since his last visit it had become almost impossible to tell Christians from other people. The religious chaos and moral relativism of our times had, as he saw it, practically engulfed the Protestant churches, except in the more remote rural districts. If this were to continue, it might be appropriate to use the word *pagan*, which originally meant nothing more than a rustic countryman, to describe these few surviving rural Christians who still "dared to be different!"

Even before the World War, a revulsion against this extreme individualistic trend was visible in liberal circles. In the idealistic philosophy itself, which liberal theology had adopted as its foundation, there was a strong emphasis upon the reality of social wholes, and the need of the individual to ally himself with some social whole, if he would achieve unity with the Absolute. In the rising science of social psychology, James Mark Baldwin had made it a truism that the individual by himself is a pure abstraction, since self-consciousness develops by a bipolar process in which the Ego and the social Other are simultaneously differentiated. In the Social Gospel movement, liberals were already urging that individualistic salvation is no salvation at all, unless the converted individual becomes a loyal servant of the social weal. But it was the World War that really broke the back of liberal individualism; for in those terrible days individualistic religion suddenly revealed its weakness and irrelevance; while multitudes of people found the moral equivalent—yes, *more* than the equivalent—for such religion in loyal, sacrificial service to "King and Country," or the "Safety of Democracy," or whatever else the war appeared to them to be about. Disillusionment followed, and individualism returned in a riotous flood; but the taste of social solidarity which came to us in the war years could not be forgotten; and it is safe now to predict that in the New Era inaugurated by the war, the social emphasis is destined steadily to grow, and any purely individualistic form of religion is bound to seem increasingly exotic and otiose.

To those of us who lived through the period of the World War, the atmosphere of these present days is very familiar indeed. There is the same sense of awe and anxiety in the presence of convulsive, uncontrollable social forces—forces which are shaking the world and threatening the underpinnings of our own dwelling-houses. There is the same sense of social responsibility.

"The world is on fire and the sparks are flying" once again, as in 1914; and none of us can wholly escape the moral necessity of girding himself for action in the emergency. Already, in many countries of the world, young men and women are rediscovering (what was well-known to the generation that fought the war) that there is a joy and an exhilaration in devotion to a cause, beside which the pleasures of a life of ease and self-indulgence look stale and tawdry. The era of self-expression is over; the vogue of *loyalty* is coming in again.

This is at once an occasion for thanksgiving and an occasion for dismay. Thanksgiving, that the moral shoddiness of the Jazz Age is at last at an end; that we are at length prepared to believe something, espouse something, do something; that life is again to be lived upon a generous and heroic scale, with far vistas in view and large issues at stake. Dismay, that the new loyalties seem to be taking the same limited form as the old loyalties of 1914, generating new antagonisms and new blind illusions which can only lead to new catastrophes and, eventually, to another wave of cynical world-weariness.

Indeed, it seems that the new loyalties are distinctly narrower and intenser than the old. German patriotism in 1914 had not half the lyric fervor and utter disregard of consequences which blind and intoxicate the Nazi youth of today. Class loyalty and class conflict before the war had nothing to match the red-hot hate and fanatical self-immolation of present-day Communists. If the old loyalties led to disaster, disappointment, and disillusionment, what will come of the new? Can we learn nothing from experience? Must we end- lessly alternate between the intoxication of narrow loy- alties and the disgust and self-reproach of the "morning after"? And must we expect that each attack of this circular insanity will be worse than the last?

Loyalty is a great good to the individual, even if misdirected. From that point of view, one can only rejoice to see the tide of loyalism coming in. Yet mis- directed loyalty is perhaps the greatest of all social ills, and from that point of view one trembles to see the rising tide. Is there a form of loyalty which is capable of blessing both the individual and humanity; which is as fervent and soul-stirring as Fascism, yet free from any taint of cruelty or meanness or hatred; which is in- tegrative and not divisive in its effects; which can com- mand the allegiance of a man without reservations and yet never violate his freedom or limit his horizon?

Puzzling over this problem, I have lately gone back for refreshment and reorientation to a book which helped me greatly in the moral crisis of the war: Josiah Royce's *Philosophy of Loyalty*. Royce's idealistic phi- losophy is at a discount today, but if there is one of his works which seems likely to survive in this age of realism with comparatively little loss of cogency, it is this. At least in the first half of the book, which deals with the challenge of ethical individualism and the problem of finding a highest loyalty consistent with freedom and with cosmopolitanism, one feels as if it had been written yesterday, with the Jazz Age and the new nationalism as its background, instead of having been written a full quarter of a century ago, before the World War.

As against the ethical individualism of his and every age, Royce makes it magnificently clear that the individual can find his freedom and realize his deepest desires only by freely devoting himself to some cause. Only thus can he find the unified purpose that will give his life drive, zest, and direction. There is no sacrifice of personal liberty or dignity in such a loyalty, he insists; indeed, the act which he takes as typical of loyalty at its best is an act of *loyal disobedience*; the act of the Speaker of the House of Commons who, when commanded by Charles I to point out certain members of the House whom he meant to arrest, knelt before his sovereign, and said, "Your Majesty, I am the Speaker of this House, and being such, I have neither eyes to see nor tongue to speak save as this House shall command." Compare the dignity of this act of loyalty with the childish petulance of most forms of self-expression, and decide in which case the individual Ego is the more highly exalted!

But if loyalty is so great a good to the individual, it undoubtedly has its perils for society. Royce recognizes this, and proposes a test by which to discriminate between good and bad causes. "A cause is good," he says, "not only for me, but for mankind, in so far as it is essentially a *loyalty to loyalty*, that is, is an aid and a furtherance to loyalty in my fellows."[6] And he proposes as his maxim, "So choose your cause and so serve it, that by reason of your choice and of your

[6] Royce, *Philosophy of Loyalty*, p. 118.

service, there shall be more loyalty in the world rather than less."[7] This is a somewhat abstract but nevertheless effective way of stating that causes whose success involves the destruction of other causes—as for example, in war—are to that extent bad, while the best causes are those whose success promotes the success of a wide circle of other causes, and so serves "the unity of all human life."[8] A man's special personal cause is ordinarily limited in its immediate scope, and its connection with world unity is remote. Yet if a man in the pursuit of such a special cause, is "loyal to loyalty"; if, while remaining true to his special trust, he respects and honors loyalty wherever he finds it, even in his enemies, then his life helps all other loyal lives and tends to create human unity in ways that are hard to trace but none the less real.

"Loyalty to loyalty"—is that the principle we need, to guide us through the stormy days that are ahead of us? Royce's critics have made fun of this phrase, as a mere platitude or a mere tautology. I think it is far more than that. If its implications were fully grasped, all forms of loyalty based upon hate and prejudice would be automatically ruled out: German loyalty which feeds upon contempt for Jewish loyalty, and erects a nation into an idol before which every knee must bow; proletarian loyalty which feeds upon contempt for the loyalties of other social classes or professions and despises truthfulness because it is a "bourgeois virtue." Yet in an age when the lower loyalties are

[7] *Ibid.*, p. 121.
[8] *Ibid.*, p. 126.

once more barking out their commands in peremptory tones on every street-corner, and the multitudes are once more responding obediently with stiff military salutes, the advocates of the higher loyalty are in a parlous plight unless they can define the object of their devotion less vaguely and more concretely than Royce has here defined it.

Even that more definite and kindling phrase which he used in his last published writings—"The Hope of the Great Community"—is still insufficient to give to the friends of the Great Community the solidarity and group consciousness which they need today, in order to make their influence effective against the pressure of great mass movements. These movements are organized and disciplined; they march in unison, under the command of a leader, living or dead; *Il Duce* in Italy, *Der Führer* in Germany, hardly less mysterious and exalted figures than the immortalized leaders whose bodies are venerated in Moscow and Nanking. How weak and futile, by comparison, is the mere disembodied spirit of international good-will and cosmopolitan fraternity, to which liberals of every stripe, political and religious alike, continue to offer up their oratorical incense! O that the friends of the Great Community could rival its enemies, in organization, discipline, unity, and leadership!

There is an answer to all this, so trite and conventional that one hesitates to offer it—an answer so often made to serve as a smoke-screen to cover a strategic retreat from the whole problem, that it is likely to be received by our intelligentsia with yawning indifference or downright resentment. *Pro Christo et Ecclesia;* that is the answer, and it is already so old that it has got itself embalmed in Latin, and embossed upon the seals of venerable, highly respectable institutions. "For Christ and the Church"! Could there be anything more insipid as a substitute for the strong wine of Nationalism or Communism! "Christian brotherhood" as a dainty remedy for class war! Ecclesiastical processions as a moral equivalent for Nazi parades! Polite exhortations in place of revolution, and prayer-meetings as a cure for economic breakdown!

Well, so be it! For my own part, I confess that I am no more deeply stirred by bishops in gaiters than by warriors in spiked helmets; and I have heard the name of Jesus used to cover such a multitude of imbecilities that I can quite understand why Professor Royce used to shy as if a missile had been thrown at him, and take refuge in cautious circumlocutions, whenever a student tried to draw him out regarding his attitude toward the Founder of Christianity. Yet I rise to remark that if there is no sense in that answer, then there is no sense in any answer at all; for one Cause that stands clearly above nation and class, and comprehends all the grand departments of human need, is the Christian Cause; and one Leader who stands clearly above other leaders—making Hitler and Mussolini look like strutting schoolboys playing soldier—is Jesus Christ.

I trust that I harbor no illusions about the Christian Church. In its existing form it is a clumsy, divided, disoriented, and appallingly tepid-tempered institution, which rarely looks the contemporary world squarely in the eye or hits straight at the heart of contemporary issues. It is involved in all sorts of humiliating compromises with social evils. Yet even in one of its most tepid and compromised branches—the German Lutheran Church—it has resisted the pressure of the totalitarian State more openly and effectively than the Socialists or Communists were able to do; and on the basis of such episodes it may fairly be questioned whether the Church is really so weak as she appears to be. After all, the Church is on a long trek. The Kingdom of God is not to be realized as the result of a Five-Year Plan. Why should she get excited? Has she not already survived the wreck of many civilizations, and many hot and hasty movements?

Suppose now that we should learn to look upon the Church, and upon Christ, with new eyes: upon the Church, not as the bulwark of respectability but as what Mr. Wells calls an "Open Conspiracy," in which all who love the Great Community are invited to cooperate; upon Christ, not merely as the gentle shepherd of the aged, but as the intrepid Leader of Youth—a leader, austere in the discipline he requires, but needing no censorship or secret police to enforce his commands, since he requires nothing that he has not first done himself, encourages adventurous initiative in his followers, and seeks nothing but the common good of all. What then? Might we not look to see, in our generation, a body of men and women yielding nothing to our contemporary political zealots in loyalty to their Cause, but resisting all forms of zealotry with strength and dignity, because they had a greater and more inclusive loyalty, beyond contamination of hate or prejudice, and had "neither eyes to see nor tongue to speak," save as their Cause commanded them?

"Is this merely," as John Bennett half-fears, "to take a romantic view of the Christian movement because everything else has seemed to fail?"[9] I hope not. I admit that, to outward appearances, the Christian movement today is not a very fit subject for romance, nor a very fit object for ultimate loyalty. It is only in its relation to the Providence of God that it gets its most compelling significance. But if our view of the Providence of God is solidly based, it should help us to a reasonable faith in the Church and its Founder, as free from romantic illusions as it is free from baseless fears.

2. A REALISTIC CONCEPTION OF THE WORK OF CHRIST

Any honest appraisal of the Work of Christ must start with a grateful recognition of the service which liberal Christianity has done in recovering the portrait of the historical person, Jesus of Nazareth. The great glory of liberalism consists in its defense of the right to absolute freedom of thought, even upon the most momentous and sacred themes, and its resolute pursuit of truth, even when it leads to perplexing and disturbing results. Nowhere has the untrammeled and truth-loving spirit of liberalism been more brilliantly justified by its fruits than in the patient "Quest of the

[9] *Christian Century,* Vol. L, p. 1406.

Historical Jesus" which began in the eighteenth century and is still going on.

The persistence of liberal scholarship in this quest of historical truth concerning the origins of Christianity was all the more remarkable, since it led liberal theology into an almost hopeless dilemma. In its retreat from the conservative Protestant faith in the infallible authority of the Bible, liberalism had come to take its stand temporarily upon the infallible authority of Jesus. The teaching of Jesus had become not only the sure touchstone for testing the religious worth of other parts of the Bible; it had become the one thing in the Bible that really mattered.[10] The figure of the historic Jesus thus took on, for liberal theology—especially of the Ritschlian school—an importance such as it had never had before in the whole history of Christian thought. *Everything* rested, like a pyramid poised upon its tip, upon the one point in universal history where Jesus of Nazareth appeared; and anything tending to cast doubt upon the truth or authenticity of his teachings would bring the whole pyramid crashing

[10] Cf. the attitude of Eugène Ménégoz on this subject: "Yes, Messieurs [he would say to his students], in this theological turmoil our refuge is in Jesus Christ. Has your confidence in Moses and the prophets, in St. Paul and St. John, been weakened by biblical criticism —that bold and indispensable science, at once so terrible and so helpful? Leave Moses and the prophets, St. Paul and St. John aside, for the time being, and go straight to Jesus Christ. . . . It is in him that you will find the one thing necessary: he has the words of eternal life. I speak to you from experience. . . . It is in Jesus Christ alone that I have found the full satisfaction of the needs of my soul: of my thought, of my feelings, of my moral and religious consciousness. Be assured that you also will find it in him." (*The Journal of Religion,* March, 1926, Vol. VI, p. 194. Article on "The Theology of Eugène Ménégoz," by W. M. Horton.)

to earth. For a time this ticklish equilibrium was maintained, since New Testament criticism seemed to result in a conception of Jesus which could, with some forcing of meanings, be made to embrace all the cardinal truths of liberal Protestantism. The "liberal Jesus" whose figure emerged from this process of accommodation is classically portrayed in Harnack's *What is Christianity?* But in the same year (1901) when Harnack's book appeared, Albert Schweitzer published the first of his revolutionary studies on the life of Jesus, which put liberal theology in the following dilemma: *either* it must admit that the Gospel records have been so tampered with that they are wholly unreliable, *or* it must admit that the teachings of Jesus were based upon an apocalyptic expectation of the End of the Age, which implied that he was "capable of error" and most unliberal in his theology.[11]

The crisis of religious thought induced by this dilemma has been very salutary, if very painful. From it there has come a portrait of Jesus different from the liberal portrait, less easily identifiable with our own ideas but more mysterious and more awe-inspiring. It is still an unfinished portrait, and no doubt will be forever unfinished; but this can be said with some confidence, that it is neither the portrait of a modern liberal religionist, nor that of a shrewd reformer, nor that of an Omniscient Deity masquerading as a man, but knowing all the time too much to take the adventure seriously. It is the portrait of One who felt the

[11] For a good brief summary of Schweitzer's contentions, see his autobiography, *Out of My Life and Thought,* pp. 48-54, 58-75.

heaped-up tragedy of our human predicament as no one else has ever felt it; who believed in the near coming of the End of the Age because he saw the Providence of God lowering like a storm-cloud over his time; who yearned over the fate of foolish and perverse mankind, wandering toward their doom like sheep without a shepherd, and interceded for them with strong crying and tears, until there came to him from God, as he believed, a message of forgiveness and deliverance for all who would receive it. Step by step, not knowing whither he went nor what the outcome would be, he followed the guidance of the Spirit in the pursuit of his mission of deliverance, until it led him to a death whose meaning and necessity he did not himself fully understand, save that it was the cup which his Father had given him to drink. The remark has sometimes been made that the world has yet to see what God can do with a man wholly surrendered to his Will. The world *has* seen; Jesus was that man.

With the clear perception of the human limitations of the mind of Jesus there has come a new and profounder estimation of his person and work. No longer is he mainly to us the Master Teacher, into whose words must somehow be read the sum of all wisdom. Nor is he mainly the Great Example, who "went about doing good" in a manner that we should endeavor to imitate. He still commands our respect as the greatest of all religious teachers, and our love as an incomparable friend to man;[12] but he commands our awe and

[12] I agree with John Baillie, that it is grotesque to combine reverence for Jesus as Son of God with a tendency to disparage his significance as a teacher. The Church has always based its metaphysical faith in

adoration as the One through whom God worked the greatest and most decisive of all His mighty acts, which turned the course of history and founded a new race of men. For us as for St. Paul, the appropriate name for him is not Rabbi, or Good Master, but Saviour.

What was the nature of this mighty saving work which was accomplished in and through the surrendered will and God-possessed person of Jesus the Nazarene? Let us be candid, and confess that it was not such as to deliver mankind immediately or completely from all its woes. Our Jewish friends are right when they remark that if by the Messiah we mean the one who ushers in the Golden Age, then it is rather strange for us to call Jesus the Messiah! Many factors in our human predicament whose importance we have been led to stress in recent days were unrecognized in his message and unaffected by his advent. He did nothing to clarify men's thinking about their cosmic environment, nothing to overcome the niggardliness of nature, nothing to solve the vexing problems of statecraft and economic organization. Aristotle, Galileo, and Karl Marx have done more for the deliverance of mankind along certain lines than he. But he did something more centrally important for human deliverance than any philosopher, scientist, or social reformer can possibly

---

the divine Sonship of Jesus upon a simple, practical faith in him as the teacher and leader who has shown us the way out of our human predicament. But in recent liberal thought this practical faith in Jesus as teacher had become so absolute that it crowded out the deeper faith in him as Saviour, and at the same time imperiled *both* faiths through the exaggeration of its claims. (See Baillie, *The Place of Jesus Christ in Modern Christianity*, pp. 99-101.)

do: he broke the power of sin, suffering, and death to corrupt and cow men's souls; and he let loose into the world a great torrent of divine life, love, and power, which is bound in the end to sweep all obstacles away before its onrush.

How and in what sense did he do this? One of the most realistic and convincing explanations of it which I have encountered in recent years is contained in a little book by Mr. F. H. Stead, entitled *The Deed and the Doom of Jesus.* The author begins by pointing out how the same great law of solidarity which under the Providence of God binds all times and places together in successive and reciprocal relations, may bind them together for evil as well as for good, so that the accumulated evil habits of individuals and groups may come at length to constitute the kind of thick-matted jungle growth of iniquity which Walter Rauschenbusch describes in his portrait of the Kingdom of Evil. The "law of succession" ordains that evil customs grow more and more automatic, in evil groups as in evil individuals, until they at length lead to destruction; but the "law of reciprocity" ordains that the better and more sensitive members of the group suffer more than the guilty ones; and their sufferings may be redemptive, if they lead to a revulsion of feeling and will which breaks and ends the bad social habit. The way of the habit-breaker is hard, for the whole mass of established precedent reacts automatically and viciously against him, and tries to do him to death; but the suffering of the innocent, like all pain, is "the reaction of health against disease or lesion," and "summons the restorative powers of the whole body to the help of the menaced or injured part."[13]

Most sensitive souls are sensitive only to a single evil, and their habit-breaking is confined to a single vicious custom—as when the monk Telemachus abolished the gladiatorial games at Rome by his heroic stand and sacrificial death. But Jesus was sensitive to the whole mass of human sin and misery, and his colossal will-power dared to defy all those social habits which were inconsistent with a perfectly filial attitude toward God and a perfectly brotherly attitude toward man. "By a transcendent exertion of the will—a will of perfect love Godward and manward—He broke the force of the world's sinful habit and made it possible for us to follow through the breach that He made."[14]

There is an objective realism in this account of the work of Christ which is in refreshing contrast to the subjectivism of liberal theology. According to the "moral" theory of the Atonement which generally prevails in liberal circles, the effect of the suffering and death of Christ is to be seen exclusively in its subjective influence upon the mind of the individual who con-

[13] Stead, *The Deed and the Doom of Jesus*, pp. 44, 45. Edinburgh, Clark, 1927.

[14] *Ibid.*, p. 55. It may perhaps be questioned whether Jesus was ever clearly conscious of so tremendous an objective; whether his intellectual horizon was not limited to the concerns of his own people. I should grant that Jesus was not clearly conscious of what he was doing. He felt more than he knew and accomplished more than he dreamed. He never dreamed, for example, of founding the Church, but he did it, by God's grace. And God's grace was able thus to work through him, because he possessed the extraordinary sympathy and feeling of solidarity which is revealed in the great word "Inasmuch" (Mat. 25:40).

templates it. That the spectacle of the Cross has still the power to stir and change the heart of a sinful individual, even across the gulf of two thousand years, is a truth that I am in no wise disposed to deny. Nor am I disposed to deny that, as Horace Bushnell said, there is an "Eternal Cross in the heart of God," and Atonement is in some sense being made in all times and places, through all sorts of people. But orthodox theology was right, I believe, in its insistence that something was accomplished upon Calvary "once for all," and need never be repeated. Three things at least were accomplished there, as I see it:

(1) A permanent change took place in the relations between God and man. God *got inside* humanity as never before.

(2) A power was permanently released and henceforth available, whereby individual human souls might conquer their sinful propensities and rise above the fear of suffering and death. This power simply *was not released* before.

(3) A new social organism, the Church, was created, through which God's Spirit and Power have ever since been mediated to human souls in a definitely new way, and in which the powers of darkness which still largely control our social life have found their deadliest enemy—a kind of benign cancer, which eats destructively into the vitals of evil institutions. This social organism *was not here* before.

The meaning of all three of these assertions will appear if the meaning of the first is satisfactorily cleared up. What does it mean to say that the relations of

God and man were "permanently changed" by the work of Christ? Does it imply anything more than that, by the supreme expression which he gave to God's unchanging love for man, *individual men* thereafter were more and more induced to change their attitude toward God, and receive the forgiveness and grace which God was always ready to impart to them? Yes, I think it means something more, and I am going to try to suggest that "something more" by telling a parable.

Consider the case of a Japanese pastor, a friend of mine, who has become so concerned about the unhappy condition of the Chinese people that he has gone to China and founded a Christian school. He loves the Chinese as if they were his own people; but he told me with sorrow that (naturally enough under present political conditions) he was never able to show the full depth of his feeling for them, and was continually thrust back into a relation of stern justice and shrewd oversight in his relations with his students. Every time he relaxes into kindness and trustfulness toward his Chinese friends, they endeavor to overreach him, he says, for they have never comprehended his real motives, and are only interested in getting from him whatever advantages he is willing to offer. So, one might say, God has been thrust back into an attitude of stern justice in his dealings with the human race.

And now suppose that one of the boys in that school in China catches an inkling of the real intention of my Japanese friend; realizes that he is neither an imperialist in disguise, nor a half-demented Santa Claus with bulging pockets which may be picked on the sly, but one who seriously and intelligently desires the deepest good of all his students—what then? The boy will suffer for it, of course. He will be first ridiculed as "teacher's pet," then ostracized and persecuted as a traitor to his country; but if he can stand the gaff, he will permanently change the spirit of that school and its relation to its founder. As one of the boys, and one who has caught the spirit of the founder, he will become a mediator and channel of influence between the master and the other boys, and the initiator of a group or movement in the school which will permit the master, at least in dealing with this group, to show the real kindliness of his feelings and enter into intimate friendly relations, without ruining school discipline and without danger of being overreached.

Such, I believe, is the rôle of Jesus in the history of humanity. Hitherto, man's attitude toward God had compelled Him to reveal chiefly the sterner side of His nature, and function as God of the plumb-line when it was in His deepest nature to be a God of grace. Some few prophetic souls, like Hosea and Deutero-Isaiah, had divined that there was something deeper than justice in God; but they had not dared to live out all the implications of their faith, and take the consequences. Jesus did. Thenceforth, God could and did draw nearer, in mercy and in power, to those who followed in Jesus' train, than He had ever drawn to mortal men before. And since God is not an individual person but an all-pervasive Spirit, He could and did do more than *draw near* to Jesus and his disciples; he *entered into* them, as Holy Spirit, and from that time on God was less transcendent and more immanent, less potential and more actual in His world than He had ever been. God "got inside" humanity in His Church in a radically new way, so that from this "colony of heaven" in the midst of a still dark and miserable world there now went forth a new power for the redemption of individuals, and a new resistance to social evils. The crowning work of Jesus was the founding of the Church, through which his glorified spirit continues the work which he began in Galilee and Jerusalem.

"Which he began," we say. But just when and where did the work of Christ begin, and *who began it?* Did it begin and end upon Calvary, in one colossal act of will-power on his part? Did it all spring from some heroic decision which he reached, some purpose which he conceived, on the Mount of Transfiguration, or during his vigil in the Wilderness, or at his Baptism, or even earlier? To ask such questions is to realize the inadequacy of every purely historical matter-of-fact account of the work of Christ; for they cannot be answered without a headlong plunge into metaphysics, an attempt to view history from above, in the light of God's Providence. From this point of view, it must be said that the work which was done in Galilee and Jerusalem did not begin in the mind of Jesus but in the mind of God. God's was the initiative, Christ's the response. Long before Jesus became conscious of his mission, long before he was born, God had purposed to

reveal Himself as Love, to close the gap of alienation between Himself and man, to "get inside" humanity as Life of its life. Yes, and must we not add that, long before the soul of Jesus began to reach up to God in eager devotion, God had begun to fashion for Himself the soul of Jesus, and set the stage for his coming? Through Moses, Amos, and the Prophet of the Exile, God was preparing the way for the Incarnation; for such a personality as that of Jesus is not made in a day. Through Alexander and Cæsar, Plato and Zeno, God was preparing the way for the work of Christ; for such an event as the Christian conquest of the ancient world does not happen without antecedents. "God, who at sundry times and in divers manners spake in time past unto the fathers by the prophets, hath in these last days spoken unto us by his Son, whom he hath appointed heir of all things, by whom also he made the worlds."[15] So said the early Christians, when they endeavored to trace to its source the river of grace which sprang forth from the Cross; and so, too, say we. The work of Christ began in God's eternal determination to reveal and communicate Himself to man; in His eternal self-communicating tendency, his "Word," which is the driving "Nisus" of all creation. The Fourth Gospel answers best of all the question when the work of Jesus began. "In the beginning," it says, "was the Word, and the Word was with God, and the Word was God . . . and the Word was made flesh, and dwelt among us." . . .[16]

[15] Heb. 1:1, 2.
[16] John 1:1, 14.

3. A REALISTIC CONCEPTION OF THE CHURCH

The conception of the Church which is implied in this conception of the work of Christ ought now to be evident. It is the conception of a social organism whose animating soul or *entelechy*, as Aristotle would call it, is the God-filled spirit of Jesus. Jesus was the grain of wheat which, falling into the ground and dying, sprang into new life in the Church. *Jesus determines what the Church is to be*, as a seed determines what the plant that springs from it is to be. The Church is destined to carry on, through the long course of history, the mighty work which God began to accomplish in Jesus' short years of ministry and whose continuance was assured with the bloody sign and seal of the Cross.

All that we have said of the work of Christ applies, therefore, to the work of the Church—except that the Church can have only one founder, one "chief cornerstone." (1) The Church continues Christ's work of mediation between God and man; it makes the life of God more and more immanent and actual in human life. (2) The Church continues the work which was so important a part of his Galilean ministry, that of bringing new power and forgiveness to individuals who are bound in the fetters of evil habit. (3) The Church continues the work which led him to his Cross, that of defying and breaking the power of evil social customs and institutions. One might go on, indeed, to note that all theological concepts which apply to Christ apply also to the Church. If God becomes manifest and incarnate in Christ, so also in the Church; if Christ has two natures, divine and human, so has the Church; if he has power to forgive sin, make atonement, and bestow saving grace, so has the Church. For the Church is the body of which he is the head, the organism through which he continues to live and act, "even unto the end of the world."

The view just defined undoubtedly has more affinity with medieval Catholic realism than with Protestant individualism and nominalism. It conceives the Church as a real metaphysical entity, something over and above the sum of its individual members, something whose life spans the centuries, something which absorbs and transforms individuals as a plant absorbs and transforms the particles of soil which it takes up into itself. I am quite conscious of the fact that in my doctrine of the Church I am more Catholic than Protestant; though I would beg leave to point out that St. Paul, the patron saint of Protestantism, held just this "Catholic" view of the Church. The usual Protestant conception of the Church as an aggregation of "elect" individuals, who seek one another's society because they have first found Christ all by themselves, strikes me as highly unreal and absurd.[17] Only through the Church do we bridge the gulf that separates us from Nazareth and Calvary. It is not unnatural, then, that I should find myself in substantial agreement with an interesting view of the Church which has lately been set forth in a pamphlet by D. A. McGregor, an Episcopalian thinker with Anglo-Catholic leanings.

[17] I realize that many Protestants hold a much higher view of the Church than this. It is among the Protestants, and not among any of the so-called "Catholic" churches, that I myself have met the

The Church, according to McGregor, is literally a "new emergent" in the evolutionary process, a new creation of God, as much above ordinary human life as that is above the life of the brutes. In the State, the Community, and above all in the Family, human life had been groping toward the new level of perfectly organic social unity, but it was in Jesus and his disciples that life definitely attained this level, and the pattern of social relationship thus set possessed the stability of a true-breeding biological species. In Jesus the new species first appeared. "Had He merely lived and passed away," says McGregor, "He would be of little interest to men today. He would have been an interesting 'sport' or 'freak' or 'mutation' in the history of humanity." He would have been like a "white rose growing on a red bush,"[18] clipped by the gardener and stuck in a vase. But Jesus was not thus isolated; he entered into social relations with ordinary humanity and, so to speak, was cross-bred into the human strain, so that now, in spite of all human corruptions, a new strain of life, a new pattern of society has been established which will breed true to type for long periods, and revert to type when apparently lost. The Church,

---

Church Catholic and learned to love her. Those who call themselves Catholics seem often to be afflicted with a most un-Catholic spirit of pride and exclusiveness. Yet I cannot forget that Schleiermacher defined the difference between Catholics and Protestants by saying that the Catholics believe they come to Christ through the Church, while the Protestants believe they come into the Church through first meeting Christ; and I have found this (to me) absurd conception very common in Protestant circles.

[18] D. A. McGregor, *The Sacred Humanity*, p. 10. *New Tracts for the Times*, No. 3. Milwaukee, Morehouse, 1934.

which represents this new strain or pattern, is as much
a novelty as was the first speck of protoplasm in an
inorganic world. It seems feeble, but the future belongs
to it, and all advance is destined to move along the line
it marks. It is as truly descended from Jesus as all
organic life is descended from that first speck of living
plasm.

> The Christian Church is the Second Humanity, its fellow-
> ship is the apex of evolution, it is the bearer of salvation and
> hope to men. . . .
> If we are to know Jesus Christ we must meet Him in the
> fellowship of the Church.[19]

This is undoubtedly a realistic view of the Church,
in the medieval, Platonic-Aristotelian sense of the word
"realistic." But is it realistic in the contemporary sense
of the word? Perhaps not, as the word is often understood. If, for example, contemporary realism's attitude
toward historical movements and institutions is correctly represented by a recent *Harper's Magazine* article entitled "How Not to Write History,"[20] then I am
far from being a realist; for the author denounces all
writers who talk about the "American mind" or "frontier individualism" as if such nebulous, unscientific expressions corresponded to anything real! Now I grant
that it is difficult to define precisely such matters as
national types and the collective characteristics of a
particular age, and for purposes of precise agreement
on matters of fact it may be desirable to avoid such

[19] *Ibid.*, pp. 8, 13.
[20] Bernard DeVoto, in *Harper's Magazine* for January, 1934, pp.
199-208.

expressions; but to suppose that an adequate philosophy of history can get along without them is, to me, as unrealistic as to suppose that the life-history of an acorn can be adequately told without mentioning the species *oak*.

When Aristotle talked about "forms" and "entelechies" he was not talking moonshine, he was talking as a good observer of biological phenomena; and if such entities as genera and species represent important aspects of reality on the biological level, how much more on the social level. Any political investigator who attempts to get and convey a realistic understanding of the contemporary Far Eastern situation without reference to that very specific self-reproducing entelechy known as the "Japanese mind" is simply stupid, and should be sent home. Again, to claim that there is no such thing as the "spirit of an age" is to exhibit a form of blindness specifically characteristic of the spirit of the age through which we have just been passing. What I am asserting about the Church is that it is a real entity of a higher type but of much the same order as "England" or "Japan"; and that the Holy Spirit or Spirit of Christ which informs and indwells it has the same kind of reality, in a higher degree, as may be ascribed to "the spirit of the Romantic movement" or "the spirit of modern science." It is no superstition to believe that individuals born into such a social organism or touched by such a spirit tend to be transformed as food is transformed by being taken up into the body. It is no superstition; it is simply good social psychology.

When I speak of the Church as a social organism with a specific entelechy, I do not mean to imply that it cannot vary from the original type. It can and has, both for good and for evil.

Every time the Christian Church has come into touch with a new cultural milieu, there has occurred what Auguste Sabatier once called a "double and mutual conversion." The spirit of Christianity has penetrated the spirit of that age and that civilization, and been penetrated by it in turn, like two species undergoing cross-fertilization; and the result has been a new form of Christianity as well as a new form of civilization. In many cases—yes, in *all* cases, in some respects—this process of cross-fertilization has enriched the very germ-plasm of the Christian Church, and advanced it toward its flying goal, of providing a form of collective life so rich and varied that it is fit to be the entelechy of the whole collective life of mankind. I am sure that this was the case when Christianity appropriated the riches of Greek philosophy; when it was cross-bred with the spirit of the Northern European peoples so as to flower out in the glories of Gothic architecture and Northern painting; or when, more recently, the scientific spirit has penetrated into the Church, to purify it of pious frauds and pious exaggerations, and make it face its task more shrewdly and clear-headedly.

On the other hand, there has been perpetual danger, in this process, that the original type of Christianity would be corrupted altogether, and the purity of the Spirit would be lost. The very vital power with which Christianity has invaded and penetrated certain forms of civilization has tempted it at length to become too completely identified with its environment; and so the decay of a civilization has superinduced a decay of Christianity. This happened with Greek and Roman Catholicism, as we all know, and it is now becoming evident that it has happened again with Protestantism. As the Roman Church decayed with the decay of medieval feudalism, and the Russian Orthodox Church collapsed with the collapse of czarism, so the Protestant churches, having become too closely identified with nationalism, industrialism, and the middle class, are declining with the decline of our Western industrial type of civilization. When what Niebuhr calls the "brief glory of the business man" is over, the glory of Protestantism may be over, too, unless it can somehow declare its spiritual independence of the peculiar type of civilization with which it has grown up.

Whenever the Christian Church has begun to decay, two types of regenerative forces have generally begun to operate: external dangers and internal schisms. As the Hebrew prophets saw in the Assyrian and Babylonian invaders the rod of the divine chastisement raised against the Chosen People for its sins, so Christian historians have seen in the rise of Islam a judgment upon the corruption of the Church. Stanley Jones remarked, on his recent tour of America, that Russian Communism was the new Islam, with whose virile and alarming rivalry God is testing and challenging the Church of today. To anyone who believes in the Providence of God, that is a remark to be taken quite seriously. One may add, that the new Paganism of

Fascist State-worship is testing the Church simultaneously from still another angle. Conceivably, of course,
the Christian Church may fail so disastrously to pass
this double test that the main line of the grace of
God will once more "go over to the Gentiles," and a
new religion will be founded which will not be Christian, but a child of Christianity, as Christianity was
the child of Judaism. But so far in the history of the
Church every great crisis of external danger has brought
forth regenerative movements within her, which have
been resisted by the sodden mass of indifferent Christians so as to result in schism, but which have been the
"salt," the "leaven," the "saving remnant" through
which Christianity has continued to survive and flour-
ish. That, it is to be hoped, will be the outcome this
time—at least in the Anglo-Saxon world, for in Continental Europe the cause seems already half-lost.

In any event, we may have confidence that the true
Church cannot perish. Churches may perish, Christianity itself may be transformed out of all recognition; but
as the Holy Spirit cannot be forever quenched, the true
Church, the Israel of God, can never perish.

> Unshaken as eternal hills,
> Immovable she stands,
> A mountain that shall fill the earth,
> A house not made with hands.

One final question may be asked about this account
of the Church, as a genuinely unique channel of the
grace of God, and a genuinely new order of humanity. The question is one that liberalism often raised: Is
it right that God should show favoritism, by picking

out any single group of people as special recipients of
His grace? Is He not the universal Father of all mankind, whose grace is equally bestowed on all? The first
answer to that, the answer which any good realist must
put first, is that *it is so whether it is right or not.* However we may explain it or justify it, the *fact* is that the
grace of God is not equally distributed. Indeed, one
wonders why there is so much talk about the maldistribution of wealth, and so little about the maldistribution of grace, which is a much greater evil, yes, the
greatest of all evils. The second answer, however, suggests a way of reconciling this apparent favoritism with
the universality of God's Providence: *it is characteristic
of the experience of divine grace to feel the impulse
to share it even if the price of sharing is persecution.*
God's elect are in a sense called to a position of privilege, but if they hug that privilege to themselves it
vanishes from their grasp. God calls His elect not to
set them permanently apart from humanity, but that
they may continue in the paths of suffering marked
out by the steps of His suffering Chosen People, and
suffering First-Born Son, thus making channels for His
grace to flow out into the whole body of humanity.

I do not mean to suggest that the Christian Church
is the *only* channel through which the grace of God is
flowing. The life of God impinges universally upon
human life, and every human institution—secular or
religious—which survives at all, survives because a
spark of the life of God is in it. If the Kingdom of God
should ever come completely on earth, it would not
simply be a magnified Church, but a cluster of glorified

institutions—States, Families, Trade Guilds, Religious Orders, and the like—of which the Church would be simply the vitalizing center and organizing entelechy. It is the function of the Christian Church to bring out the divine spark in other institutions, other movements, and *other religions*, by entering into commerce with them all, opposing their sins and arrogances, helping them define their true functions, communicating to them the breath of the Spirit which is needed to fan into flame the spark of God which is in them. What an amazing burst of flame has the Spirit of Christ brought up out of the spark of God in Hinduism, in modern times! What a burst of flame might come from Nationalism and atheistic Communism if the Christian Church dared to go to Calvary in their midst! But today, in her corrupt condition, the Christian Church is not fit to shoulder the Cross, not fit to be the Saviour of the World. She must and will undergo judgment and purging to fit her for her task.

CHAPTER V

A REALISTIC PLAN OF
SALVATION

THE whole course of our discussion up to this point
would be relatively fruitless, if it did not issue in some
plan of action. It would be a very unrealistic theology,
indeed, which, after depicting the perils of our human
predicament and after summoning all possible divine
resources and reinforcements, resigned its task before
answering the question, "What then shall we *do*?" Yet
it is inevitably with much trepidation that one ap-
proaches this final decisive phase of the argument. It
would be so much more dignified, so much safer to
one's intellectual self-respect, to "sign off" after analyz-
ing the elements of the situation, and say, like President Hoover's Commission on Social Trends, that the
best any group of theological planners can do with the
data now in hand is "to lay plans for making plans."

Shaking off this purely judicial mood of cautious
tentativeness, as a relic of the easy-going age of liberalism, and bracing ourselves for the act of decision
which our sterner age requires, let us now in this concluding chapter endeavor to map out a plan of salvation which will be adequate to the situation in which
we find ourselves. And since the first requirement of
every good plan of action is a definite *aim*, let us begin
by considering what would be a practical *goal of salvation* at which the Christian Church of our generation

should aim, in view of all the difficulties she faces, and all the resources she possesses.

1. THE GOAL OF SALVATION: THE KINGDOM OF GOD

There is an ancient and perennially significant name for the Christian goal of salvation, a name whose meaning has changed repeatedly with the changing exigencies of the time, but which will continue to be the most stirring battle-cry that Christian lips can raise, so long as the Church shall last. It was the name which Jesus used to designate his own dearest hope, and so long as we continue to pray the prayer that he taught us, we shall center our thoughts and our desires supremely upon it. I refer, of course, to the *Kingdom of God*. There is probably no better way to define the aims which should govern the endeavors of the Christian Church today than to inquire what meaning should be attached to this ancient battle-cry in our own times.

Robertson in his *Regnum Dei*[1]—a rather old book, but still one of the best guidebooks in this field—has pointed out that three different interpretations of the Kingdom of God have been held by Christians from early times, sometimes simultaneously, sometimes in opposition to each other: the Kingdom of God as an inward state of mind, realizable here and now by individuals; the Kingdom of God as an ideal social order on this earth; and the Kingdom of God as a state of

[1] New York, Macmillan, 1901. See p. 119. I have revised Robertson's list of principal interpretations, giving first place to the monastic idea of the kingdom "within," to which he gives only casual mention, and grouping together as second in my list the millenarian and theocratic ideas, which he puts second and third.

perfect beatitude in heaven. All three of these conceptions follow naturally from the root idea of the *Kingdom*, or better *Kingship* of God; *i.e.,* the *rule* of God's will, which Christians pray may be "done on earth as it is in heaven."

During the period of liberalism, the idea of the Kingdom of God tended to become secularized and humanized in a peculiar way. Under the influence of the idea of Progress, the hope of a steadily increasing earthly happiness almost completely obscured the hope of heavenly beatitude—even for those who still professed belief in immortality—while the faith in man's ability to procure this happiness by his own intelligent efforts made the phrase "of God" tend to drop into the background. When men talked of "getting together to bring in the Kingdom," when they preferred to speak of the "democracy of God," instead of the "Kingdom of God," the relationship of man and God in the New Testament conception of the Kingdom was reversed. God and not man was now the "silent partner" in the undertaking. Human Providence sketched the plans, but God was invited to lend a hand, if He would, in order to speed up the job. Faith in God, like faith in immortality, was an article in all liberal credos, but many held it tentatively on a pragmatic basis. God was important in so far as His power "worked" as a useful aid to Man in the important human undertaking of "building the Kingdom." All in all, it might have been better to speak of the "Kingdom of Man" instead of the "Kingdom of God."

Realistic theology reacts against liberalism (and its

offspring humanism) at both the points just mentioned, and tends to revert to a more traditional conception of the Kingdom of God. It tends to regard it as God's Kingdom, not man's, governed by an often inscrutable Providence whose workings man must humbly seek to discern, if his small efforts are to count at all; and it tends to doubt whether the perfect consummation of the Will of God is ever going to come to pass within the sphere of earthly human life.

It would be too much to say that we are now going through a great revival of the hope of the life everlasting; although John Baillie's very able and eloquent book[2] is undoubtedly a portent of the times. Realists of Reinhold Niebuhr's school tend to be definitely suspicious of the belief in immortality, having imbibed sufficient Marxism to feel the force of the charge that immortality is an "opiate" that dulls the revolutionary ardor of the masses. Realists of Henry Nelson Wieman's school tend also to be suspicious of this belief, as a form of unregenerate self-assertion and wishful thinking, which ought to be laid aside by one who aspires to completely disinterested love of God.

Realists must undoubtedly beware of everything that looks like an "escape mechanism" or an encouragement to a "defeatist" attitude; but if they are what Tillich calls "belief-ful realists," they are bound to consider the question to what extent mundane reality points beyond itself to a transcendent realm of reality. To acknowledge the reality of God's transcendent activity in Providential judgment and redeeming grace, and

[2] *And the Life Everlasting.* New York, Scribner, 1933.

then refuse to "*hope* in God," is self-contradictory. If there is a Divine Life that is the eternal source and eternal condemnation of all imperfect human lives and institutions, then man's final destiny *must* be found in some form of union with this Eternal Life. And, needless to say, all evidence that individual survival of death is a real fact must be sympathetically considered.

When I thus suggest that the revival of some form of the hope of eternal life is a feature of realism, I speak only for myself; but when I suggest that the scaling down of earthly hopes to more modest proportions is characteristic of realism, I speak for the whole movement. Neither for the individual nor for society does realism expect perfection on this planet. As Paul Tillich said recently, realism differs from Tertullian in his famous opinion that "the soul is naturally Christian"; it thinks the soul is not naturally Christian but naturally pagan.

That does not mean that human nature is wholly bad, but it means that the victory of spirituality over natural sensuousness and natural egotism is an incomplete victory, and the "perfectionist" who claims to be completely sanctified is usually the victim of unconscious hypocrisy. This conclusion gets its greatest force, however, from the perception that, as social beings, we are continually participants in the collective sin of the various social groups to which we belong. The man who claims to be impeccable is usually blind to the sources of his income, and blind to the fact that he continually profits by the collective egotism of the nation or class to which he belongs. To one who views the behavior of the contemporary national State with a realistic eye, the prospects for the complete harmonization of the interests of rival social groups look very remote, indeed. As a Christian, one cannot seek less than the redemption of society; as a realist, one is bound to view its professions of repentance and vows of amity with a degree of incredulity.

"But if we may not aim at perfection on earth, at what on earth *may* we aim?" The question is a natural one, but it involves a false dilemma. It implies that if complete perfection is unattainable, there is nothing worth striving for. A similar popular misunderstanding exists with regard to the pursuit of truth. Because absolute certainty of ultimate truth is humanly unattainable, the conclusion is drawn that there is no certain truth at all, that we can rest our lives upon. Neither conclusion follows from the premise to which it is attached. In a world where human knowledge is always relative and partial, we may nevertheless arrive from time to time at halting places in the pursuit of truth, where the ground is firm under our feet and the landscape stretches out below us so wide and so far as to give us, so to speak, a foretaste of omniscience. And in a world where human attainment forever opens up new difficulties and new problems, we may nevertheless experience (both in our individual and in our collective life) moments of genuine *deliverance*, so glad and so decisive as to give us foretastes of the divine perfection. Perhaps it was such moments that Jesus had in mind when he spoke those startling words, "Be ye therefore perfect, even as your Father which is in heaven is perfect."

Every type of civilization, every period in history expresses its foretastes of perfection in some characteristic way, which is conditioned in part by its characteristic evils and imperfections; and this accounts for the many variations which have occurred in the idea of the Kingdom of God—especially in that aspect of the idea which has to do with earthly society.

To the early Christians, the Kingdom of God implied a great levelling-down and evening-up of all the injustices of life, in which God's oppressed and persecuted minority would come into power, not by their own strength but by a great cosmic convulsion. The expected convulsion never occurred; but by a process of peaceful penetration the Christian community honeycombed and undermined the Roman Empire, and the persecuted minority actually did come into power. It was natural enough that when this unexpected triumph occurred, the Christians concluded that the Kingdom of God had come, accepted the rulers of the Christian Empire as God's vicegerents, and settled down into a subservience to the political State from which, in the Eastern Orthodox churches, they have never escaped.

In the West, matters took a different turn, and a different conception of the Kingdom of God resulted. The Christian Empire was first threatened, then submerged under a wave of barbarian invasion. All seemed lost, and in the gathering gloom of the Dark Ages it was hard to believe in the Rule of God. But in the twilight of the ancient world, just after the sack of Rome, St. Augustine's voice was raised in prophecy. The Earthly City might perish, he said, but the City of God, the Church, would never perish; and in her continuance she would save all that was worth saving, since whatever of stability and justice the Earthly City possesses is due to the presence of the City of God within her. The prophecy came true, in the main. The Church won an ascendency over the barbarians, through the love and courage of her missionaries, which the Empire was unable to establish with all its legions. The Church preserved the germs of ancient culture in her monastic establishments during centuries of dense ignorance; and when the time was ripe, these seeds bore fruit in the second great social triumph of Christianity: the architecture, philosophy, poetry, and ordered feudal society of the thirteenth century. This time, it was the Church and not the State which Christians identified with the Kingdom of God; for truly, God seemed to be administering the affairs of Europe through His earthly representative, the Pope, in whom the whole pyramid of the feudal system found its apex.

This triumph, as we know, was temporary like the first. Perfection never finally arrives—thank God!—in human affairs. The feudal order decayed, and the Church with it; until in the eyes of Luther and many others, the Pope came to represent Antichrist instead of Christ, and the idea of the Kingdom of God as a theocracy under ecclesiastical control was badly shaken. In the Lutheran churches, the hope of an earthly social order which could in any sense be called the Kingdom of God was totally abandoned, and the idea was restricted to the inner life and the world to come. In the Calvinistic churches, the hope of an earthly theocracy survived, and concrete attempts were made to realize it, at Geneva under Calvin himself, in Scotland under the Covenanters, in England under Cromwell, in New England under the Pilgrims and Puritans; but the attempt to bring about the Kingdom of God by legislative enactments has never been successful. A long list of obsolete, unenforceable "Blue Laws" is all that remains of these attempts. Generally speaking, the smaller Protestant sects have been conscious of this difficulty, and have therefore not attempted to realize the Kingdom of God outside of their own limited fellowship.

There is much in the present plight of Western civilization to remind us of the days of St. Augustine. The civilization which took its rise in Europe four centuries ago, which spread all over the earth in the age of discovery and colonization, and which won universal prestige through the scientific and industrial achievements of the nineteenth century, has come to seem to us as much a part of the order of nature as did the Roman Empire in St. Augustine's time. Its familiar ideals of free investigation, free competition, free trade, free speech, have come to be truisms in the minds of educated men. And yet today, barely twenty years after it reached the peak of its glory, this civilization threatens to succumb to external and internal forces which have loosened its whole fabric, and put many of our most cherished values into jeopardy.

In Asia, the tide of rebellion against Western ideas is steadily rising, and Japan stands forth as a first-rate military power, capable of breaking the hold of the West upon the Far East. Within Western society itself, the capitalistic economic order and the democratic form of government are working so badly that revolt against them is widespread. Both the Fascist "totalitarian State" and the Communist "dictatorship of the proletariat" are definitely opposed to the principles of individual freedom of thought and speech upon which all the culture of modern times is essentially based. It is not hard to understand why "freedom" is a bad word to Fascists and Communists, since it has often in practice meant no more than the claim of business to immunity from social control of any sort; but with the disappearance of freedom in Russia, Italy, and Germany, what we used to call "modern civilization" has been overwhelmed as truly as Roman civilization was overwhelmed by the barbarians. In Latin America, we are told, optimism about democracy and internationalism still prevails, in spite of minor wars and civil disturbances; but throughout the greater part of the world today, the civilization which seemed irresistibly advancing, twenty years ago, is now on the defensive, and men are asking, as they did in St. Augustine's day, whether there is anything to cling to in a world that is going to pieces.

The Kingdom of God, for men of our generation, is bound to have social implications. The economic and political crisis in which we find ourselves is too vividly realized as an essential part of our human predicament, for us to be able to be satisfied with any purely "inward" or "spiritual" Gospel. Our message of salvation for the individual must not be unrelated to the task of salvaging whatever is of value in our disintegrating social system, and preparing the way for a better one. No one is truly "saved" whose life does not help upbuild a world-order more fraternal than this. At the same time, it is evident that this social task is a long and difficult one, which is not going to overcome international war, racial injustice or class discrimination within the present century, or doubtless many centuries to come. If the individual is to be courageous enough, serene and well-poised enough to continue to work for the common good through the long period of confusion and transition which lies ahead of us, he must have resources which outward failures cannot touch, and transcendent objectives beyond the flux of contemporary events. There must exist for his vision a transcendent pattern of justice in the paternal relation of God to all His children; and he must be able to realize this pattern on a small scale in the life of the Church, the home, and the community.

It should be the aim, then, of the Christian Church in our time to prepare and announce the coming—by shreds and patches, no doubt—of a communal world civilization of which God's relation to His true sons is the best pattern: a civilization to which existing nations, races, and classes are capable of making distinctive contributions, as is every individual and every group, but which will not be under the egoistic domination of any. History has taught us that this ideal, grounded as it is in the structure of reality, is nevertheless not capable of sudden and total realization, as the early Christians supposed. Neither is it realizable through any ecclesiastical theocracy, as the Roman

Catholics and the Puritans supposed. It demands for its realization a common consent on the part of *all* the fundamental human collectives—states, families, trades and professions, etc.—which is infinitely hard to obtain. Yet to resist the encroachments of concrete private and sectional interests against the universal interests of the invisible Kingdom, to collaborate with every agency that makes for the common weal, and to help individuals and small groups to live even now as if the Kingdom had already come, is infinitely worth while, and this is the task of the Church. By what methods and policies she should be guided under present conditions it is our next and final business to consider.

2. THE SALVATION OF THE INDIVIDUAL

The Christian Church must continue to preach the ancient Gospel of individual salvation in this and all coming generations. The special exigencies of our time make the need of this Gospel more pressing than ever, if possible, for the individual seems now to be in peril of being completely swallowed up in the mass as so much cannon fodder, or so much energy for production, or—the acme of meaninglessness—an unemployed "hand" waiting for a job, and consuming so many cents' worth of food per day while he waits. In such a time, it is exceptionally difficult but exceptionally important to preach "reverence for personality" and "the infinite worth of the human soul," and to broadcast to the discouraged multitudes the news that a life of inward serenity and power, a life of victory over self and circumstance, is still possible.

It has been interesting to note how the old concern for individual salvation has been coming back, by a circuitous route, in these recent years. We started out, just after the war, to consign evangelical religion to oblivion amid a chorus of scornful merriment, led by the editorial staff of the *American Mercury*. "Sin" and "duty" we decided were two mid-Victorian prejudices of which every healthy mind must rid itself, lest it succumb to cramping inhibitions and develop a morbid complex of some sort. "Principles" and "standards" were hang-overs from Puritanism; all such fixities were out of place in a purely fluid and relative world, where the only reasonable rule was to laugh at taboos and "try anything once." What we found out, in exact proportion to the thoroughness with which we revolted against moral standards, was that a life without clear aims was a thoroughly footless, meaningless life, which tended either to fly wildly into fragments or to lapse into unutterable boredom. If we did not exactly recover our sense of sin, as a consequence of this perception, we at least became conscious of a yawning emptiness in our lives, a sense of frustration and futility; and we enabled the psychoanalysts to earn substantial incomes in our frantic efforts to get reintegrated and readjusted, and find an aim in life. For it became evident, the longer we struggled with our sense of futility, that we could not escape from it so long as we remained self-centered. Happiness, we saw, depended upon inward harmony between our warring desires; and since some at least of these desires were social, we could not be individually "integrated" unless we were socially "adjusted" and had some socially worthful purpose which "took us out of ourselves." With this principle once established, there was no longer anything except prejudice to prevent us from accepting the evangelical doctrine that no man can be saved except through self-surrender. The quest for self-expression had come full circle, and brought us back to our starting point.

Perhaps, on second thoughts, it was a spiral and not a circle. We are very near indeed to the evangelical position, but the language of the old evangelism has lost its appeal for us. We admit that we ought to integrate our drives in such a way as to satisfy our need for recognition and response; it never occurs to us that this is what the evangelist means when he tells us we must be "converted" and "forgiven." This misunderstanding is natural, for there was much in the old evangelism that was artificial, false, and unrelated to the real needs of real people. An adequate evangel for today must spring out of a realistic understanding of human nature. It must begin where Dr. Richard Cabot begins, in his fascinating discussion of *The Meaning of Right and Wrong*: with the perception that the great moral imperatives are laid down in the biological and psychological structure of human beings, and the structure of the world in which they have to live.

Cabot starts with the assumption that fulfillment of desire is a perfectly legitimate human aim; but he takes only three or four steps of realistic logic from this point of departure to the conclusion that something like conversion is needful for every human being. Certain desires are more authoritative than others, for they follow the lines of our fundamental make-up, and express what we really *need*. A characteristic of our nature is our need "to hang together," which means "to be organized around a plan as bodily organs are"; and this integrity of character, once achieved, survives only "by facing reality, that is by dovetailing with the facts around us."[3] From this demand to "face reality," in ourselves and in the world, a straight path stretches to the stirring conclusion of the book, where the "ultimate desire" is described as a demand for some objective End to whose supreme requirements we may rightly subordinate all lesser desires:

Our central need pushes us towards wholehearted activity, in art, science, sacrifice, creative love, and religion. . . .

When that moment comes, any son of Adam knows that for this chance he has been waiting or pushing all his life. At last he is face to face with the Real Thing. Once we used to call this Real Thing the hunger and thirst after righteousness. That sounds priggish and self-righteous now. But the plain facts of human psychology are more inflexible than the fashions. The plain fact is that nothing is so deep in us as the passion for an opportunity that will bring the whole of us into action. Most of the time we are a dozen removes away from that. We dawdle along at a snail's pace. We peck and pull at a corner of our job. But when the chance comes to give all that is in us, and to risk all for what we love, then we know that we have met our need, and that for this end we came into the world. . . .

Every one of us was made to act whole-heartedly for some minutes or hours before we die, and so, as we go edging forward, like an amoeba, now one bit of our hopes and now another, a sense of frustration grows up in us. Our divided mind hungers to escape into unanimity. Are we to be forever

[3] Cabot, *The Meaning of Right and Wrong*, Chapter III, "Needs."

tongue-tied and speechless, forever packing our trunks but never starting, forever criticising our twisted minds with a mind still twisted, forever selfishly trying to be less selfish? If we are used to calling the universe by its Christian name we can pull ourselves together and face Reality in prayer. But even prayer is imperfect because it needs to prove its sincerity in action. At our best we escape into a whole-hearted deed.[4]

Is it sufficient, then, to say that individual salvation or "escape" is to be found in *any* whole-hearted deed, *any* consuming devotion to which all lesser desires are subordinated? I do not think Dr. Cabot means to imply any such conclusion. Whole-hearted self-giving to some Reality beyond ourselves is the indispensable condition of salvation; but it is possible to go disastrously astray at this point, and give oneself to that which does not deserve the gift. Through such shortsighted self-giving, which treats relative goods as though they were absolute, and blindly idolizes them, it is possible to get the "moral equivalent" of a religious conversion, without truly meeting the Ultimate Good.

All veracious war novels, from *The Four Horsemen of the Apocalypse* to *Mr. Britling Sees It Through*, report miracles of moral transformation to have been accomplished by the outbreak of hostilities, which enabled many frustrated individuals to escape from amorous entanglements or personal weaknesses into the freedom and joy of a "whole-hearted deed" of sacrifice. I have been told by a keen observer that some young Nazis, when they enlist in the service of the Swastika, do so with the fervor and sincerity of Chris-

[4] Richard C. Cabot, *The Meaning of Right and Wrong*, pp. 433, 436, 437. New York, Macmillan, 1933. Quoted by permission.

tian converts, and experience a great heightening of their moral powers. Now there may be among them those who honestly seek in and through their service to their country to serve the universal good, as Donald Hankey did in the World War. I would not deny that such men have met what Cabot calls the Real Thing, and found genuine salvation; though I think they are bound to become disillusioned about the human object of their faith. But the peril is, in our time, that men will lay themselves, bound hand and foot, on the altar of some such Moloch of nationalism, and lose all faith in any higher object of devotion. It cannot therefore be too strongly emphasized that no one is justified in giving himself without reservations to anything that means less than *the total good of all, including himself.* Only God answers to this description. Only God, the source of all good, can be trusted to treat individuals "always as ends in themselves, and never as means only." Nations and classes, unfortunately, cannot be trusted. They are willing to consume gluttonously as many human sacrifices as may be offered them, and howl for more.

To say that God is the only possible author of salvation, the only adequate object of dependence, is perhaps not very helpful, unless one goes on to say where God is to be found. I think it is plain from the outcome of our previous discussion, on Christ and the Church, where we must locate God. God is manifest to a degree in the order of nature; and men like Spinoza who worship Him only there, are not far from His Kingdom. He is manifest to a higher degree in the

rough justice that destroys civilizations when they become too unfraternal; and men like Marx and Lenin,
who revere this trend toward communal living without
calling it "God," are also not far from the Kingdom.[5]
But the inner truth of God's nature is most clearly manifest in the Spirit of Christ, the Spirit in the Church. He
who is least in the kingdom of the Spirit has found a
personal salvation which laughs at the bounds Spinoza
set to human happiness, and quite exceeds the scope
of the Five-Year Plan.

For a classical expression of the meaning of the
Spirit, we might, of course, go to the New Testament,
and read St. Paul's list of the fruits of the Spirit, or
his panegyric of love, the greatest of them all; we
might take special note of the depth of *Koinonia*, "fellowship," which the Spirit created among the early
Christians, binding them into a unity like that of the
body and the members, the vine and the branches. But
these examples are so familiar as to have become shop-
worn, and they seem to suggest that the Spirit is something archaic and strange, whose manifestations ceased
with the age of the Apostles. To my mind, there is no
better modern example of the meaning of the Spirit
than that which is afforded by the Society of Friends.
I recognize, of course, that the Friends had many pe-
culiarities, which might easily have wrecked a religious
movement that had less of spiritual depth and poise;
and I hold no brief for that severe disparagement of
the sacramental and traditional elements in Christianity

[5] For an expression of Marxian faith in the inexorable trend of
history, see the concluding paragraph of Trotsky's *My Life*, cited by
Niebuhr, *op. cit.*, pp. 128, 129.

which sets the Friends in such flat opposition to many other Christian communions. With the passage of the years, however, these eccentricities in the Quaker type no longer seem centrally important, being, indeed, treated rather lightly by most modern Friends; while the bareness and plainness of Quaker worship and Quaker manners make the essential Christianity of the Quaker spirit stand out in bold relief, like a fine old face in a plain antique frame. What that spirit was, and still is, in Quakerism at its best, I find most clearly expressed in the remarkable words of James Naylor:

There is a spirit that I feel that delights to do no evil, nor to revenge any wrong, but delights to endure all things, in hope to enjoy its own in the end. Its hope is to outlive all wrath and contention, and to weary out all exaltation and cruelty, or whatever is of a nature contrary to itself. It sees to the end of all temptations. As it bears no evil in itself, so it conceives none in thoughts to any other. If it be betrayed, it bears it, for its ground and spring is the mercies and forgiveness of God. Its crown is meekness, its life is everlasting love unfeigned; it takes its kingdom with entreaty and not with contention, and keeps it by lowliness of mind. In God alone it can rejoice, though none else regard it. . . .[6]

Here, I believe, we have the Eternal Gospel in its depth and breadth, and in its utter simplicity. All that is absolutely essential to salvation is that *this spirit* should permeate human life, from center to circumference. Sacraments may help to convey it, social science may help it to express itself more effectively, political action may be necessary to get it embedded in

[6] Cited from p. 26 of the compendium on *Christian Life and Thought in the Society of Friends*, published as the "First Part of Christian Discipline" of the English Friends. London, 1922.

laws and institutions; but these things are secondary, while the Spirit is primary. They are means of grace; it is the very substance of Deity. It is the Holy Spirit, the Spirit of Christ, the Spirit of God; and the Good News of the Gospel is that it may, under certain conditions, be communicated to men, who are then lifted above their sin and weakness to become sharers in the patrimony of the sons of God.

The chief of these conditions is a simple one: that we should enter into a relation of intimate fellowship, in worship and in work, with those who already possess the Spirit—or who, as they would prefer to say, are possessed by it. It is a simple condition, but a searching one, for no one is at home in the fellowship of the Spirit who is not ready to follow its guidance; and the guidance of the Spirit, though it leads to joy in the end, is contrary to the promptings of the most clamorous and imperative of our human impulses. Whoever would follow the Spirit must deny himself and take up his cross. Most of us do not yield to that demand without a struggle. Most of us deceive ourselves when we suppose that we have yielded. Yet the Spirit does not leave us to ourselves; it offers itself freely to our rebuffs, returning good for evil without either resentment or self-righteousness, until at length it "wearies out" that element in us which is "of a nature contrary to itself," and we cross over from the side of the crucifiers to the side of the crucified. After that, we may betray the Guide to which we have given ourselves, and may act from time to time as if we belonged to ourselves, but we can never entirely get away from its influence, and never be happy again in the old life. We have met that for which our souls were made, and we know it.

By thus insisting upon *fellowship* as a prime requisite for individual salvation, I do not mean to imply that the power of the Spirit is confined within the walls of churches, nor that ecclesiastics are capable of keeping it under lock and key and dispensing it at will. Now that the spirit of divine love has become incarnate in the human race through Christ and the Church, no barriers can confine its influence. There are families and neighborhoods in which the Spirit palpably dwells. But no individual can continuously pursue so remote and difficult a goal as the Kingdom of God unless he is upborne by a fellowship of some sort. He flags from time to time in his devotion to the ideal, but there are others whose enthusiasm rekindles his. He fails and grows discouraged, but there are others who hearten him. He has his besetting sin which often unfits him for service; so, indeed, have all, but *not the same sin*. Little by little the members of such a group repair each other's deficiencies by the silent contagion of personal influence, which operates most effectively between comrades in a common cause; while over all there is the controlling pressure and reinvigorating power of the group mind, which is the mind of the Spirit, revealed often clearly in moments of communal worship. Whatever we may think of the special methods and theories of the Oxford Group Movement, I think we may agree with them that the working unit of personal religion is not the individual, and none of the more massive forms of church organization, but the *intimate group*, sharing experience and looking together for guidance.

In a previous book (*A Psychological Approach to Theology*) I have pointed out that among the great influences making for a revival of personal religion in our time is the growth of the mental hygiene movement and the development of our knowledge of human nature and human needs. The more realistic our knowledge of people becomes, the more certain are we that they need forgiveness and renewed moral power as much as their ancestors did; and the better able are we to minister to their deep need, *if we have the resources.* But I should like to make it plainer that I did, perhaps, in that book that an objective source of power, beyond the needy person and beyond the "case worker" or pastor who is trying to help him, is as necessary and important as it ever was. There is no such thing as salvation by pure technique. There is only salvation by the power of the Spirit, proceeding from God through Christ and the Church. Psychological technique can render inestimable service in diagnosing the difficulties of the needy individual and clearing away certain artificial obstructions that wall him off from the life of the Spirit. But unless he somehow comes into touch with the Spirit, and is caught up into its larger life, he will have to continue to limp along with half of his powers unmobilized, uneasily conscious that he has not yet met the Real Thing for which his soul is groping.

3. THE SALVATION OF THE SOCIAL ORDER

In discussing the means of individual salvation, we have found ourselves taking what might be called a tone of confident conservatism. This is justified, I think, by the fact that in every generation, from the very start, the Christian Church has known pretty well how to change the characters of individual men by bringing them into touch with the Spirit of Christ. In spite of all overstrained asceticism and all bungling appeals to fear and self-interest, the Church has gone on producing saints and martyrs almost in spite of herself. But it cannot be claimed that the Church has ever been equally effective in the social sphere. The story of her efforts in this direction has been magnificently told by Troeltsch in his *Social Teaching of the Christian Churches and Groups*; and it is on the whole a rather disheartening story. With sickening regularity, learning little from past mistakes, she has continued to go astray in two opposite directions: *either* she has maintained the purity of her ideals by washing her hands of all worldly concerns, thus leaving society in the hands of knaves and scoundrels; *or* she has boldly and officially taken a hand in politics, thus involving her ideals in all sorts of petty compromises with special interests and parties. Either she has been so unworldly as to be negligible, or so worldly as to be despicable; and in both cases she has always grown restive and repentant after a while—and fallen into the opposite extreme!

Perhaps it is inevitable, in one sense, that the Church should perpetually oscillate between an attitude of world-denial and world-affirmation, opposing society most vehemently when it is most opposed to her principles, then becoming partly reconciled with society whenever it shows some slight symptoms of being reconciled with God. A variable "tension" of this kind is perhaps the only possible relationship between a transcendent religious ideal and the world of temporal affairs. Yet the extremes of unworldliness and worldliness are pretty clearly pernicious, and the thought cannot be banished that these hasty oscillations from one extreme to the other betoken a sort of nervous uncertainty on the Church's part as to what she is, and what function she has to perform. Might not a little clearer thinking on this point help to steady her nerves for the present crisis, and make her better able to promote the social good in her own characteristic way?

We have seen in a previous chapter that the Church exists to continue and complete the ministry of her Founder, who came to seek and to save the lost individual, to announce and actively to demonstrate in his life the coming of a New Age of more fraternal social relations, and finally to bring man and God into relations of filial love and trust. Unless the Church preserves the continuity and purity of these aims and of the Spirit which nourishes them, she is no longer a Church, but only a sanctimonious sort of political machine. There is therefore a good *prima facie* case for preferring the extreme of unworldliness to the extreme of worldliness. Better for the Church to be a persecuted minority, a saving remnant in a hostile society, better for her to be crucified with Christ, than for her to curry favor with the political powers that ordered the crucifixion—and would order it again straightway, did any such heroic "habit-breaker" loom again today on the horizon. Let us see first, then, to what extent the Church can contribute to the salvation of society while remaining a purely spiritual and non-political institution.[7]

1. *In her efforts to form and transform the individual, in producing strong, self-reliant free agents, devoted to the common good, the Church is rendering a great service to society.* A society composed of moral ciphers or "yes-men" is not an ideal society. It sounds paradoxical, but I dare maintain that *the individualism of Protestant Christianity*, its ability to produce independent characters, "obeying God rather than man," *is in one sense its greatest social asset.* Strong-minded individuals, when possessed of a social conscience, are a permanent menace to evil social institutions. The solitary conscientious objector, who politely but firmly says "No" when asked to violate his religious principles, may under certain circumstances become a "social habit-breaker," like the Founder of Christianity; and the more he is made to suffer for his non-conformity, the more effective is his protest.

2. *There is power in the "foolishness of preaching."* Simply to *proclaim* the Kingdom of God, as the final authoritative ideal for life, is to accomplish something. It is to do what Washington once advised doing, at a critical moment in this nation's history: to "raise a

[7] The following pages owe much to Henry Hodgkin's *Christian Revolution*, especially to the chapter on "The Way," which has been reread with one eye on Niebuhr!

standard to which the wise and honest can repair." In a world that is deafened with partisan battle-cries and imperiled by the cynical "wire-pulling" of all sorts of selfish and sectional interests, it is a boon to have one institution at least devoted to the *total and eternal good of all mankind*, and steadfast in her proclamation of it as the final goal toward which all human effort must tend. Simple preaching of the word of the Kingdom is much; but if in addition to this, as Charles Clayton Morrison suggests, the Christian cultus takes up the word from the preacher, and makes it the theme of hymn and prayer and sacred ceremonial, then the word has double power, for it sinks deep into man's emotional nature and gives him something of the poet's urge to create some form of beauty in which to embody what he has felt.

3. *The fellowship of the Church can provide a foretaste of the meaning of the Kingdom of God, and a demonstration of its present possibility, at least on a small scale.* This seems to have been the chief feature of the strategy of Jesus, so far as he had any "strategy" at all. He took a small group of followers into intimate fellowship with himself, and lived with them as if the Kingdom of God were already present. As that fellowship has grown, it has quietly undermined and destroyed all sorts of social "walls of partition," like that between "Jew and Gentile," or that between "bond and free." Slavery and race prejudice are not automatically destroyed in society when they are ignored in the fellowship of the Church; but they are weakened to that extent, and a leaven of ethical discontent is created

which perpetually works toward a more unified social order. The invitation to "whosoever will" to come into the fellowship and partake of the Lord's Supper, to sit down together at a common table, the most intimate and respectful of all forms of social intercourse, is in itself a triumphant act of defiance thrown in the faces of those who claim that human unity is an unrealizable ideal.

Stanley Jones tells of an incident that occurred in his *ashram*, where a group of Christians drawn from many races and castes gathers every year during the rainy season "to live as if the Kingdom of God were come." A part of their discipline was to take turns doing all the necessary work of the camp, including the emptying of the slops—a form of work which in India is supposed to be done only by outcaste "sweepers." When the sweeper of the camp was for the first time relieved of his disagreeable task by a man of a higher caste, he was overcome with amazement. That night he appeared outside Mr. Jones's window in the moonlight, his hands pressed together in the Indian gesture of adoration; and Mr. Jones avers that as he looked into the face of that sweeper he saw the birth of a soul. It is impossible to miss the profound social implications of such an incident. With every social outcaste received into full and genuine Christian fellowship, a blow is dealt at all systems of social and racial discrimination. It is true that many of these discriminations have invaded the Church; but when the body of Christ is in a state of health, it casts out these poisonous invading influences as a healthy organism throws off disease germs.

4. *By its charities and its missions, the Church relieves many of the acuter forms of human distress, and corrects the maldistribution of privilege to a considerable extent.* In so doing, the Church reverses the process of egoistic accumulation and selfish exploitation which is so characteristic of ordinary human society. It is as true today as it was in the time of Christ that the ruling class in society tends to "lord it" over other mortals, and takes extreme satisfaction in the accumulation of possessions and privileges which are its spiritual mark of distinction. Your genuine Christian, on the other hand, is made uncomfortable and restless by the realization that there are those who are hungry while he eats, ignorant while he is educated, socially outcaste while he belongs to the élite; and it is the perpetual endeavor of Christian service in its various forms to share one's privileges as universally as possible, first of all with the neediest. If this disposition were prevalent in all members of the ruling classes, war and violent revolution would become forever unnecessary, for the rulers would be as eager to share their advantages as the disinherited are to claim their rights. Christian missions are the real "moral equivalent for war"; if all men had the spirit of the best missionaries violence might be reduced to a minimum in human affairs. The best missionaries are not only willing to give charity out of their superfluity, they are willing to lower their standards of living, give up their social status and all the privileges that birth or education has conferred

upon them, if they can only bring health, or knowledge, or the light of the Gospel to those who have missed these benefits through no fault of their own. I need hardly add that what we call the "missionary spirit" is not confined to the sphere of foreign relations; the best type of social settlement work exemplifies the same spirit perfectly.

So far we have carefully skirted the borders of politics, and confined our attention to the non-partisan forms of Christian activity. From the point of view of the Lutheran and other purely "spiritual" churches, there is little more to be said. To seek to mold public opinion through sermons on public questions, or through ecclesiastical pronouncements on public issues, is beyond the province of the Church, according to this view. To be strictly consistent, the "spiritual" churches ought to discourage their members from holding public office or from mingling at all in secular affairs—as is the attitude of the Mennonites, for example.

Yet this deliberate flight from the whole political sphere is bound to insulate the Church increasingly from the vital concerns of mankind in the age of political strife and change which is upon us; and it is no longer possible to pretend that political questions have "nothing to do with salvation." As we saw in Chapter II, it is now clear that neither the scientific conquest of the niggardliness of nature nor the religious conquest of individual sinfulness can deliver mankind from its real predicament, unless accompanied by some political transfer of property and privilege which will make it possible to administer the goods of earth in the interest of all instead of in the interest of a limited few. Every attempt of the Church to help individuals leads her at length into the political sphere—as occurred in the case of the liquor problem—and all attempts at relieving social misery which stop short of the redress of political injustice fail to get at the deep source of the disease they set out to cure. The disinherited classes are increasingly contemptuous of the Church's efforts at charitable amelioration of their distress. "We want no condescending saviors!" they shout. "We don't want charity; we want justice!"

How are we to answer them? Are we to plunge the Church once more into the thick of the political fray, and fight for the dictatorship of the proletariat as the Crusaders fought for the Holy Sepulcher, or Cromwell's Ironsides fought for the Christian Commonwealth? I cannot believe that well-exploded error in policy should be repeated. When the Church identifies herself with any political party or social class, she divides her own fellowship, and cuts off her own power at its source. When she lends her official sanction to violent coercion, whether it take the form of international war or of revolutionary insurrection, she throws away her own characteristic weapons, which are the weapons of persuasion. As Vincent Nicholson says, "Attempts at persuasion by a group that stands committed to ultimate coercion, are crippled from the outset."[8] The Spirit does not cry or strive in the streets, it does not quench the smoking flax or bruise the broken reed; and the

[8] Vincent D. Nicholson, *Coöperation and Coercion as Methods of Social Change*. Pendle Hill Pamphlets, No. 1.

Church must keep the purity of the Spirit, or it is no Church at all. It would seem, then, that the Church is in a strait betwixt two evils: either she must do nothing in the political sphere, and fail to serve mankind at the point where its need is just now the sorest; or, since all political activity is ultimately coercive, she must sanction coercion and lose the persuasive power of the Spirit.

Is there any escape from this dilemma? I see no easy or simple one; yet I believe it is possible for the Church to serve the cause of political justice without losing her own soul or compromising her principles. The Church as an institution should maintain an absolutely non-partisan stand, I believe, but should judge the platforms and actions of partisan groups fearlessly, whenever they clearly go counter to the general good, and set forth as plainly as possible, in non-partisan terms, the basic principles of social justice. Such a non-partisan stand is difficult to maintain, because as a matter of fact the Church is protected by the powers that protect the existing social order, and draws its financial support from the existing economic system. Until the Church can contrive to *declare its independence* of the present order of society, the taunt of its radical critics will have a bitter sting: that the Church discourages revolutionary violence, but accepts the protection of a society which maintains its privileges by violence!

I see no way for the Church as a whole to declare its independence at once of the system on which all our institutions now must rely for support; but I believe there is a great need in our day for modern religious orders living in a state of voluntary poverty and gaining by the manner of their life the right to speak with freedom and utter frankness to all parties in the contemporary conflict. Such a group is the *Christa Seva Sangha*, an Anglican religious order which has played a great part in the Indian struggle for political justice.[9] I wish we might have Protestant religious orders in this country, which would be free to go farther in the direction of severe self-discipline and political action than the Church as a whole can go. Perhaps the *Fellowship of Reconciliation* and the *Fellowship of Socialist Christians* may be regarded as examples of what I have in mind. Bill Simpson would be a much more significant figure if he were a member of such an order, instead of a solitary eccentric. What can be accomplished by such orders for the reconciliation of divergent interests in industrial strife and the breathing of a better spirit into the conflict might perhaps be illustrated by the recent work of the Society of Friends in the coal fields, where by winning the confidence of all parties they have done at least as much for industrial justice as all the agitators and investigators whose efforts have been reported in the newspapers. Conceivably, some such politico-religious order might actually

[9] See *The Dawn of Indian Freedom*, by Father Jack Winslow, the head of this order. I have just received a pamphlet from my friend Mr. C. C. Liang, describing the founding of a somewhat parallel religio-political Christian community in Mu Ping district, Shantung Province, China. This community, known as "Mt. Zion in China," will be supported entirely by its own labor and voluntary gifts, and so will be sufficiently detached from the social order in China to serve it disinterestedly and impartially. It proposes to devote itself, among other projects, to rural reconstruction.

break the existing deadlock of conflicting interests, and find the true way to a classless society.

In addition to all this, the Church should encourage her members to train for positions of political leadership, and should recognize that intelligent performance of the duties of the citizen is an essential part of Christian duty. The Church cannot dictate the political opinions of her members, but she can train their political intelligence by providing a forum for the discussion of public questions in the spirit of mutual tolerance and good-will. One thing she should make clear: that in the realm of politics there is need to heed the Scriptural injunction to be "wise as serpents and harmless as doves"! Christians in politics are apt to be well-meaning bunglers. Because their own motives are honest, they are apt to believe too much in the honesty of the motives professed by interested groups. Because their ideals are above the average, and they find these ideals practicable in private relationships, they are apt to try to enact these counsels of perfection into the laws of the State—with the result that hypocrisy, evasion, and nullification destroy all the fruits of their endeavors. Because they abhor violence, they are apt to be indecisive in public crises, when any decisive move is almost sure to be accompanied by violence. The Christian statesman ought to understand fully, before accepting office, that it is not his task to bring in the millennium, but rather to estimate shrewdly the relative force of the various selfish interests which converge about him, and by playing them off skillfully against each other

secure the highest degree of justice that is possible under the circumstances.

Into this difficult and delicate work of balancing
selfish interests, the Christian statesman may enter with
a good conscience, for he has the highest of all precedents, the example of God Himself. If our account
of the Providence of God is not too far astray from
the truth, God operates in the political sphere as truly
as in the sphere of the inner life. The stern hand of
justice does not reveal His nature as deeply as does
the open hand of grace; yet it is by these two hands,
working together, that God accomplishes His great de-
signs in human affairs. Both hands are divine; the State
is as necessary as the Church; all observation goes to
show that some form of political or economic pressure
is needful to bring about any great social reform.

One grave misunderstanding needs to be avoided
here. God's political policy may be stern, but it is not
violent, nor does it follow the maxim that the end jus-
tifies the means. The simile of the clenched fist is misleading if taken too literally. God's way of dealing with
His adversaries is less like pugilism than it is like jiu-
jitsu; He makes them overthrow themselves by the force
of their own onslaught; He makes them attack and ex-
terminate each other like rival gangs of gunmen; He
stands sadly and firmly upright, holding the plumb-
line, and they pitch head-foremost at His feet through
overreaching themselves and losing their balance. The
Christian statesman or citizen who tries to follow the
divine leading in this difficult game of politics will not
be a man of violence; though where violence is already

pitted against violence he will know how to manipulate these forces, "backing the devil of vengeance against the devil of greed," as Reinhold Niebuhr suggests. He will not try to destroy armaments nor stop strikes unless he is prepared to put some better instrument of justice in their place; but seeing the evils that follow in the train of *all* wars and *all* forms of civil commotion, however just in their intention, he will make it his constant endeavor to win by persuasion, conciliation, and genuine agreement what is never so well won by coercion. He will be especially eager to develop scientific, non-partisan diagnoses of our social ills, and new methods of "non-violent coercion," like those so dramatically employed in India by Mr. Gandhi, which will tend to mitigate the hatred and malevolence of group conflict and raise it to a plane where each party holds the other in chivalrous respect.

Is it too much to hope that, by Christian social action and Christian statesmanship, Western civilization may yet be delivered from its grosser injustices without total collapse, and without passing again through a Dark Age in which most of the values of art and science would be lost? I am entirely persuaded that there exists a clear pathway to social salvation without violent revolution, and that the Church can help to lead the way to it, if she acts wisely, vigorously—and soon! Some of the ways in which she may wisely act have already been enumerated: through her regular non-political forms of ministry, tending to ameliorate extreme social injustice and elevate the plane of social conflict; through advance-guard groups which will be freer to declare their independence of the present social order than the whole Church can be, and free to espouse specific programs of social action while remaining in fellowship with their brother Christians who espouse other programs; through Christian citizens and Christian statesmen who try to guide public policy into the most ideal channels possible, while candidly and realistically reckoning with the very *unideal* factors that control the public mind and will. In all these ways the Church can render real service; but to stop at this point would be to overlook a most essential service which she can render in the present crisis: *She can change the public mind and will, and so bring about otherwise impossible changes in public policy.*

The power of the Church to mold public opinion and stimulate the morale required for collective effort and collective sacrifice is universally recognized in wartime, when statesmen make every effort to capture this power and prostitute it in the service of merely national ends. It is to be hoped that in future wars, international or civil, the Church will not be sold again into any such Babylonish captivity as she endured in the World War, when she showed herself pathetically eager to fiddle any tune that the State might call.[10] But there are ways in which the Church may use this great power of hers for the common good, without stepping outside her proper sphere at the bidding of selfish interests or harebrained fanaticisms. *Her proper sphere is precisely the sphere of the mind and will, collective as well as individual; and she is as competent, in a crisis, to*

[10] See *Preachers Present Arms*, by Abrams.

convert a nation's soul as to convert an individual's.
The task of straightening and strengthening the perverted mind and will lies in her peculiar province; the inertia of the public mind and the paralysis of the public will are the basic cause of our steady drift toward social chaos. Without social science and political agitation, the Church alone cannot check this drift; still less can *they* check it without the Church. She cannot herself discover the precise economic mechanisms by which our present absurd state of poverty-in-plenty is to be overcome; that is the task of social scientists; but she can demand of the social scientists the sort of scheme which really answers to the requirements of social justice, and she can create public interest in every scheme that seems to meet these specifications. She cannot herself directly engage in the work of transforming the blueprints of the social scientists into political programs and legislative enactments; that is the function of political parties and movements; but she can create a public passion for reform, a public intolerance of selfish and dishonest politicians, and a willingness, more important in peace-time than in war-time, to sacrifice sectional interests for the general good. She may rightly stigmatize as a "slacker" any supposed Christian who is indifferent to politics in such a time as this, and demand that everyone relate his private activities to the public service in some fashion, direct or indirect—whether as part of the scientific "air force" which soars above the battle and maps the path of advance, or as a humble participant in the many-sided drive for a saner and juster society, which plows from

trench to trench and eventually smashes through to the next great objective in the endless march toward social salvation.

Let us be less rhetorical and more concrete; the urgency of the times requires plain speaking. The situation in which we find ourselves in the world today is simply grotesque. If Dean Swift had had sufficient prescience to divine in advance the kind of tangle we have got into, and had sent his Gulliver to our world to report upon it in another chapter of the immortal *Travels*, our forefathers would have shaken their heads and averred that this time the Dean had gone too far. That there should be nations of pygmies and giants and human-like horses is plausible enough, if you let your imagination run on a holiday; but that men should mourn over a bumper crop and sigh with relief over a drought, that they should produce so many goods, with the aid of marvelous mechanical slaves, that they all became impoverished together, that they should . . . but why go on? . . . the story is obviously beyond the bounds of verisimilitude! Yet that incredibly irrational world is the world we have; and it is the Church's first business, obviously, to make plain to all parties concerned—that is, to everybody—that in the name of the God of reason and of righteousness, this nightmare must not be allowed to last. Inability to better the situation may be excusable; but willingness to continue it and defend it, because a few people profit by it, is inexcusable; and the Church must make this very plain.

Next, a word in season to the economists and other

social scientists. The Church must make it clear to them that they are no longer entitled to public support unless they bend every nerve to the task of finding a rational way out. Ponderous tomes proving that nothing can be done, clever dialectical arguments that demolish every constructive plan of escape and conclude by offering us a choice between Fascism and Communism—that is, between two alternative ways for reason to abdicate in favor of passion and violence— against such pronouncements of our learned guides the public wrath is beginning to rise, and the Church must warn them of it. Let them produce something better than any social device now in the field—something better than the aimless drifting and superficial tinkering that *are* leading us to Fascism or Communism—or let them hold their peace. If they are really helpless, it may be forgiven them; but let them confess their helplessness with due humility and due appreciation of the human tragedy that is involved. Let them not proclaim their intellectual bankruptcy with an air of superior intelligence, and look down their noses at anyone who is so naïve as to make a definite proposal. That kind of intellectual snobbery and dilettantism may have been appropriate in the age of liberalism, now past; it will not be possible for long in the age of realism.

Finally, a word to the general public, including both the financial "ruling class" and the more or less exploited "man in the street." The Church must point out to both of these groups the necessity of effort and sacrifice on their part if the evils of our present situation are to be overcome. If they wait for the economists to produce a solution so rational that it hurts no one's interests, and costs no labor to attain, they will wait forever. If they wait for the government to transform itself and us without severe pressure from public opinion, they will wait forever. A peaceful revolution, by way of the ballot box and basic legislation, costs far less than a violent one; but still it costs something, especially to those who now are in the position of privilege. To the mass of the disinherited, the Church may well point out the difficult position of our present rulers—who are mostly not "robber barons" but harassed and well-meaning trustees—urging that they be treated with every mark of personal consideration, and greeted with public esteem instead of with scornful vituperation when they have the grace to submit to demotion in the social order. To the ruling class itself, the Church should address an appeal for generosity and public spirit. Such an appeal would be grounded in the fundamental Christian faith in the presence of a better self in every man; and in many great crises of the world's history there have been those who have answered to it, blazoning on their standards the motto *Noblesse Oblige*. Coupled with this higher appeal there might well go on an appeal to enlightened self-interest; for it is plain that business cannot revive and fortunes must continue to evaporate unless the purchasing power of the great mass of the population is somehow restored; which cannot be done unless the bankers relax their stranglehold on the money-supply. Against those who refuse to respond to such appeals, and persist in upholding a disgraced system with a callous unconcern that says "After us the deluge"—against public enemies of this sort, the Church must speak in tones that crack and sting like a whiplash: "Out! Out of the halls of government! Out of the lobbies of Congress! These halls were to be sanctuaries of justice, but ye have made them dens of robbers!"

Among the bewildering variety of proposals that are being made for the cure of our diseased social system, there is one which seems to me to be unusually significant as a test of the sincerity of every citizen or public servant who claims to love the public good; and for this reason alone the Church should take a special interest in it. It does not claim to be a complete program of social reform; but it does claim to be a scientific remedy for the chronic shortage of money which keeps the greater part of our population poor in the midst of plenty. I refer to the so-called "Social Credit" plan of Major C. H. Douglas, which provides that the quantity of money and credit in circulation be based upon an annual accounting of the real wealth of the nation, in terms of goods and services, instead of being based upon an arbitrary quantity of metallic currency and the decisions of private bankers; that the annual appreciation in national wealth due to the steady increase in mechanical efficiency be distributed in part through a proportional price-discount based upon the excess of production over consumption and designed to stimulate buying—retailers to be reimbursed out of the national credit for the discounts they grant; that the balance of the annual appreciation be distributed in the shape of an outright dividend, in which every citizen shares alike, whether he be employed or unemployed, rich or poor. For the details of this ingenious proposal, and arguments as to its economic feasibility, I must refer the reader to other and better sources.[11] I only desire here to point out its moral and religious significance. Granting its economic soundness—for which so good a social thinker as the present Dean of Canterbury is ready to vouch—then it follows that it is possible for us *tomorrow*, if we have the mind and the will, to pass over from our present order of scarcity and poverty into a new "economy of plenty," where the poor are no longer with us and man is set free forever from economic slavery, through the increasing efficiency of his servant the machine. *If we have the mind and the will*—aye, there's the rub; but it is the Church's great task to create in us the mind and the will through effectively presenting to us the contrast between what we are and what we might be. In the Social Credit scheme, I believe she now possesses a kind of minimum standard of social justice which every Christian might be educated to uphold. Other measures no doubt will be necessary, as the new problems of the economy of plenty emerge; more radical programs might well be advocated by pioneering groups within the Church; but I find it hard to see how anyone could deny to humanity-at-large the future fruits of mechanical invention—given a suitable system of estimating and distributing these fruits—without proclaiming him-

[11] See the chapter on "The Basis of Exchange" in *Christianity and the Crisis*, edited by Percy Dearmer. London, Gollancz, 1933. For a longer exposition, very well written, see *Economic Nationalism*, by Maurice Colbourne. (London, Figurehead, 1933.)

self an enemy of the race for which Christ lived and died, and for whose material needs he assured us that God was concerned. No genuine Christian, I believe, could take such a stand; hence, the Church might well uphold *either Social Credit or something better* as her minimum standard of social morality.

I have spoken, of course, as though the Church were prepared to take the lead in this social emergency. Actually, she is not; and many of the severe words of judgment which I have put into her mouth would rebound upon her, if uttered. Before the Church can exercise authority over men, she must get right with God. And this brings us back finally to a point which cannot be too often emphasized: The primary duty of the Church is not to do good to individuals, nor to exert pressure upon groups, as if she herself were man's chief hope and stay. Man's chief hope and stay is the Providence of God. The great quality to be demanded of the leaders of the Church is not Herculean will-power, nor Ulyssean shrewdness of wit, nor even humanitarian compassion, but a capacity to discern and communicate the Word and the Will of God. On this primary prophetic function of the Church, all her other functions depend; without it, they all fail. Only *God*, working *through* Christ and the Church, is adequate for individual and social salvation.

Let us set our minds straight upon this cardinal point, by considering a parable of human effort and divine resource:

There was once a tribe of Indians in the Far West, living in a desert not many miles from the foothills of a high mountain range. Their great need was for water; for their land was naturally fertile, and whenever it rained the desert blossomed overnight. So they prayed ardently to the rain-gods, and they danced wildly before the rain-gods, cutting themselves with knives till the blood flowed; but they never got more than a light shower. And there arose certain atheistic critics in their midst, who muttered against the medicine men, and doubted the very existence of the rain-gods, and claimed that if ever they were to have water, they would have to rise up and get it with their own two hands. These enterprising humanists devised little hand-carts, in which they carried water for miles across the desert, to water their little gardens. But still the desert was a desert.

Now it happened at length that explorers visited those parts; and they noticed that there was a great lake high up in those mountains, whose waters were cut off from the desert by only a little ridge of rock. So in the course of time came a group of settlers, and blasted a passage in that ridge of rock, and led the water across the desert in a network of irrigation ditches. And today the desert is no more a desert, but "blossoms as the rose."

It was the glory of the scientific age which lies just behind us that it learned how to chart the vast resources of nature, discern the lines of connection that link us with these resources, and then build connecting channels through which nature's abundance flowed out to meet our need. I cannot believe that the social problems of the age that lies ahead of us are to be solved in any other way. They will not solve themselves if we pray to God, beat our breasts, and let things drift as they have been going. They cannot be solved by human cunning and human will-power alone, though these must play their part. We shall be delivered from our social ills only if we first learn how to discern behind the surface of human events the constant action of divine Providence, and then learn how to align ourselves with the great thrust of that holy Will, and serve as instruments in that mighty Hand.

INDEX

Abraham, 54
"After Liberalism—What?" John Bennett, ix
Aids to Reflection, Samuel T. Coleridge, 26
Alexander the Great, 141
Amaziah, 98
America (*see* United States)
American Journal of Theology, 33 *note*
American Literature: A Period Anthology, Oscar Cargill, 11 *note*
American Mercury, 164
Ames, Edward S., 35
Amos, 101-106, 141
  denunciation of, 98
  realism of, 97
Andover-Newton Theological Institution, x
Anglo-Catholicism, 143
Aristotle, 134
  on biological phenomena, 146
Arminianism, 16-21
Asia, rebellion against West, 160
Atlantic Monthly, 71
Atonement, doctrine of the, 118, 136, 137
Augustine, St., 16, 19, 74
  on Christ and Church, 117
  prophecy of, 158, 160

Baillie, John, 155
  on Jesus as teacher, 133 *note*
Baldwin, James Mark, defines the individual, 122
Barth, Karl, 5, 13
  influence of, 36
  liberalism of, 33

Barthianism, 34, 37
Beckwith, Clarence A., 35
Belief Unbound, W. P. Montague, 58, 59 *note,* 115
Bellamy, Joseph, 21
Bennett, John, 33 *note*
  on American theology, 2
  on facts, 114
  on optimism, 25
  on romanticism in religion, 130
  on the new orthodoxy, 9
Berkeley, George, 19
Bill of Rights, 22
Biological phenomena, 146
Blue Laws, 160
Boodin, John E., 12
Book of the Twelve Prophets, The, George Adam Smith, 98 *note,* 103
Brown, William Adams, place in liberal movement, 33 *note*
Browning, Robert, 4
Brunner, Emil, 13, 37
Buckham, John Wright, 30 *note*
Buddhism, 46, 118
Burt, Struthers, faith in God, 91
Bushnell, Horace, 16, 25, 34, 86
  on the Atonement, 137
  theology of, 26-31

Cabot, Dr. Richard, on need of conversion, 165-167
Cæsar, Julius, 141
Calvary, work accomplished on, 137
Calvin, John, 80, 160
  belief in Atonement, 118
  belief in predestination, 81-83
  on temporal authority, 93